THE SOMME, 1916

A Personal Account

Norman Gladden

SAPERE BOOKS

THE SOMME, 1916

Published by Sapere Books.

20 Windermere Drive, Leeds, England, LS17 7UZ,
United Kingdom

saperebooks.com

ISBN: 978-1-80055-615-7.

Dedicated to the memory of
My Dear Comrades
Privates Downs, Bryant, Taylor and Corry
of the 7th Northumberland Fusiliers

and of My Mother
Evelyn Mansfield Gladden
representative of the Women on all Home Fronts
who endured immeasurable agonies from the
absence of their Menfolk
on Active Service in
the First World War 1914-18.

TABLE OF CONTENTS

ACKNOWLEDGMENTS

Grateful thanks are due to Dr Christopher Dowling and Miss Rose E.B. Coombs of the Imperial War Museum for supplying helpful advice.

PREFACE

This work is based on the personal diary which, as a private in the infantry, I kept during service at the front in the First World War. Though in general diaries were forbidden, evidently it was not considered that they constituted a danger to security. Many serving men must have kept diaries of this sort but none came to my personal notice. A number have certainly survived.

My original entries were brief memory aids rather than detailed descriptions: dates and times were noted, but names of persons and places left to be added later, so that my pocket-book, had it fallen into the hands of the enemy, would have been of rather less interest to him than, say, the normal letter from home, inevitably to be found in Tommies' pockets.

The diary had a second stage when, during the years immediately following the war, the individual entries were expanded while the actual events were fresh in my memory. Even in this extended form the resultant picture was too disjointed to be suitable for publication and the eventual emergence of the chronicle in narrative form went through a number of stages before it emerged in three parts under the tide *Full Pack*. When *Ypres, 1917*, Part II of *Full Pack*, was published by William Kimber in 1967, on the fiftieth anniversary of the Ypres battles, I added historical notes at appropriate points in the text to put my very personal viewpoint in the wider context of the war, and the work's definitive form can be said to have been reached. Part III was issued in similar form as *Across the Piave*, by HMSO for the Imperial War Museum in 1971.

The present volume comprises the hitherto unpublished Part I of *Full Pack*. In my opinion it is the most devastating part of the story, due largely to the fact that it culminates in the final stages of the great Battle of the Somme in the autumn of 1916 when the front was bogged down in the mud and the operations had become a slogging match with the elements as much as with the enemy. The units in the line were disorganized and depressed, and if hopes of victory before the winter were still voiced here and there, it was not with much conviction.

This personal story has not been fictionalized in any way: this is how it appeared to one of the hundreds of thousands who took part in the epic Somme battle, each of whom experienced his own war, in many ways similar but in even more ways differing from those of all his comrades. The events described are set down in the order in which they occurred, and nothing relevant has been omitted. My object has been to present the war as it appeared to me at the time, to present myself as I was, and not as I would have liked to be.

On both sides there were many brave men in this terrible battle, only a few of whose deeds have been set down in history's chronicle; there were many of the opposite types whose misdeeds and omissions are best forgotten; but it would be true to say that the majority were just ordinary men, usually young and with little experience of life, generally patriotic and desirous of doing their duty to the land of their birth, their homes and loved ones, but naturally frightened and fearful of being maimed or killed. The writer speaks for the majority, remembering always that we were all individuals each with his own particular faults, fears and foibles. A dwindling band of erstwhile allies and enemies form a surviving brotherhood of those who were there, having learned at least the lesson that to do one's duty in defence of one's beliefs and the common weal is something we can only reject at the expense of our peace of mind.

Whatever we may think of life we do know that the dead in this great upheaval, for which they had little or no responsibility, completely fulfilled their mission. We continue to remember and to salute them.

January 1974
E.N. GLADDEN

I: PRELUDE

On 4th August 1914, following an ultimatum that Germany should cease violating the territory of Belgium whose neutrality we had covenanted to guarantee, Britain declared war on the German Empire. The Great War, which had now become a frightening fact, had indeed been widely forecast, although the actual event still came as a surprise to most of us. Not long previously there had been played in London's West End a melodrama, *An Englishman's Home*, which in fact — not having yet become a habitue of the theatre — I had not seen although I had read much about it in the newspapers. I also remember well how the theme of invasion by German troops wearing *Pickelhauben* had been frequently featured in boys' magazines, of which I owned a varied collection. The public certainly had not forgotten the 'build more dreadnaughts' drive, and Lord Roberts's campaign for conscription to meet even such an emergency. Some had read Robert Blatchford's *Daily Mail* articles 'Germany and England', of 1909, which were republished at the time.

But, as everyone has since read, 1914 had been a lovely summer and we had all had much else to distract us. This was especially the case of a young man, such as I, who had left school the year before, a month or two before his sixteenth birthday, to become a temporary civil servant as boy clerk in the Post Office Savings Bank in Blythe Road, West Kensington. With reasonable prospects of achieving by examination the security of a permanent position in the Civil Service, it was natural that the insecurities of the age should have had less impact upon my imagination than the manifest wonders of the world around me. Balloon-filled skies at weekends and the advent of the aeroplane already foreshadowed the conquest of the air. A still undiminished belief in the inevitability of progress, in the better meaning of the word, and a burning faith in the civilizing mission of the great British Empire.

Only a congenital pessimist could have felt, at least up to 3rd August, not merely that the bright Edwardian Age, which we could discern around us and indeed appreciate for its unbounded promise, but also Western civilization itself, which had disseminated its gifts around the earth in an abundance such as no previous civilization had managed to achieve, were about to commit suicide. And all this apparently because one of the most advanced of the European communities had for ruler a short-sighted Kaiser filled with false pride and unwilling to exert, at the crucial hour, pressure upon events well within his competence, which could have placed the European nations on a cooperative course that could have led to a stable world. Germany was already ensured of commercial supremacy without war, but the small man with the decisive initiative, wanted something more romantic and, at an immeasurable cost to civilization, in the event was both to lose his throne and to ruin his country.

That summer the sun had favoured the seashores of our islands. As recently as July I had accompanied my father and a friend to Bournemouth, where we were excellently catered for at a respectable boarding house for the modest charge of one guinea each for the week. The seaside in those days was gay with stalls, bathing machines, sideshows and concert parties. In the special case of Bournemouth there was also the Winter Garden with its large orchestra, at that time paying a good deal of attention to the new ragtime. I can still, across the years, hear the strains and rhythms of 'Alexander's Rag-time Band' and 'You'll Have to Get Under, Get out and Get Under'. The latter referred to the joys of the new-fangled motoring craze, which, on numerous music-hall stages elsewhere were also being guyed by the popular comedian, Harry Tate, in his sketch 'Motoring'. Practically every town had its music hall, some more than one, where usually twice nightly the man-in-the-street for a few pence could enjoy a programme of histrionic and musical talent, much humour and usually a good deal of vulgarity.

The following week, my mother and sister, who had visited Bournemouth, on their return to town were caught up in traffic dislocations due to troop movements connected with mobilisation.

I first came into contact with the ferment that was taking place in more thoughtful quarters when I went to Trafalgar Square during that fateful weekend and found myself present at a demonstration against the war, which was being staged by pacifist bodies mainly of the left, whose pleas on this occasion proved so unpopular that the demonstrators would have been badly manhandled by the crowd had not the mounted police intervened. Certainly I did not find their arguments very convincing for there seemed to be no doubt at the time whence the aggression was emanating. The moment of choice was past.

We were well placed in our home in Earl's Court Gardens to visit the neighbouring exhibition, to enjoy the side-shows and bright lights, to mingle with visitors from far and wide, and, on Saturday evenings, to watch the firework displays from the banks of the artificial lake with its famed watershoot, which I never cared to try, despite occasional free tickets. The White City at Shepherds Bush was an even more extensive and magnificent version of pleasure ground, peculiar to the age, with greater facilities for combining the normal amusements of such places with exhibition halls for more serious trade and subject shows. As a member of the carefree crowds that thronged those bright and pleasant terraces on the Bank Holiday of 3rd August, I was not alone in my inability to sense the magnitude of the tragedy that lay ahead.

It happened that the following day was not only to be our day of destiny, it was also my seventeenth birthday. I did not then expect to be actively involved in the fighting, which would surely not last so long — or so most of us thought. Although intensely patriotic, a strong sense of realism prevented my regretting the probability of an early end to hostilities, which caused so many of my compeers to falsify their ages, in some cases by a number of years, in order to be accepted for the army in advance of their nineteenth birthdays.

I was not completely ignorant of army routines for when I was still in elementary school I had joined a Kensington Scout Troop, which was on the point of being converted into a cadet corps. This meant its acquiring a military-style uniform with puttees, and arming with obsolete carbines of Boer War vintage by the War Office. I had then learned to form fours and to slope arms — not 'shoulder arms', as I had previously thought — and to march in column of fours. The scouting I had looked forward to, for it was all the rage at the time, influenced by Baden Powell and the weekly boys' magazine, *The Scout*, but I took little interest in army drill and decided to detach myself before I became too involved. A natural shyness, coupled with a nervousness which caused me to jump a mile at any unexpected bang, had always spoiled for me the real fun of letting off fireworks. Such proclivities were calculated to diminish any attractiveness that military pursuits might otherwise have held.

I went up to town on 4th August, and never shall I forget the reactions of the vast crowds surging round the old Queen's memorial in front of Buckingham Palace on that momentous evening, a spontaneous manifestation of jingoism which literally took one off one's feet. A normally sensible populace seemed to have suddenly gone mad. Every song and melody with the slightest patriotic allusion — some of Boer War vintage which I had not heard before — was sung with gusto. There was 'Good-bye Dolly Gray', of course; this must have been the first song I had ever heard, almost before I was out of my cradle.

In response to repeated shouts from the crowd, King George V came out on the balcony of the Palace, to be greeted with sympathetic cheers and thunderous applause. Very impressive was the singing of the national anthem taken up spontaneously by many a thousand throats. The passing of a number of gun-carriages into the Mall marked the culmination of this great excitement, and it would hardly have been human to suppress the shiver of pride that ran down my spine. There seemed small reason for misgiving at the time. Were we not shielded by the vastest and most powerful navy that the world had ever seen? And did not the spirit of Nelson still guide and guard our national destiny?

It is easy today to look back with horror at that display of mass chauvinism, and to pity the poor fools of military age in the crowd who would, before it was all over, be called upon to pay a disproportionate price for our folly. Fully to understand it one must turn back into that moment of history, to see the world as it then appeared to us, and to have absolutely no foreknowledge of what was to happen upon the morrow and all those sad days that were to follow. This, even the best informed among us can never do, and many who have tried have fallen so ludicrously short of the truth that one is bound on the evidence to doubt the validity of everything that has been set down after the event.

I shared completely in the general excitement, read with avidity the news from the front, suitably garnished by busy journalists who had suddenly found themselves in clover, and was immediately horrified by the tales of civilian intimidation and terror perpetrated by the new Huns, as the Germans were quickly labelled. Such reports, which are sometimes today discounted in the name of fairness, if often exaggerated, were sufficiently authenticated as in accordance with the enemy's admitted policy of ruthlessness which he honestly believed would help to shorten the war — 'being cruel to be kind' as it were.

I felt a great and justifiable pride at the news of the early battles and the retreat from Mons, in which our small but highly trained regular army of Contemptibles, as they were labelled by the Germans, covered themselves with glory. I followed with continuing interest the often scrappy and usually inaccurate accounts of those battles whose names figure on memorials set up after the war in towns and villages throughout the land — the Marne, Le Cateau, Loos, Neuve Chapelle, Ypres and the highly dramatic opening of the disastrous attack upon the Dardanelles. Recruitment from the beginning was so overwhelming that the authorities were unable to cope with the human tide and for some months organization fell far short of requirements.

Immediately upon the outbreak of war there was a run on cash deposits which fell with full force upon my Department, the Post Office Savings Bank. For a few days this kept us on overtime at the office until eight and nine o'clock each night and, quite apart from our natural patriotic fervour, this opportunity to earn a little extra money was widely welcomed, even though the boy clerks' rate was only 4½d an hour. But the scare soon faded when reason had returned, and then the daily routine went on very much as before. Our views on the future were soon modified, and before the first war Christmas had come and gone we were accepting as true Kitchener's warning that our hopes for an early decision were totally unfounded. The war itself was rapidly becoming a routine to which our normal habits would have to conform. Yet none but the congenital ultra-pessimists ever thought that we might be defeated. This attitude was sustained by a widely based national self-confidence that must seem completely irrational in the seventies, but was powerfully bolstered up — or would have been had such bolstering been needed — by a sense that defeat to our island nation would be so dire that death would be preferable.

Even before the first bombings from the air, carried out initially by the vast Zeppelin airships, which had occasionally sailed over the land in the days of peace, the business-as-usual attitude to the war, initially assumed by the Government and the trading community, were radically changing. At the time, these attacks — so much less devastating than those of the later war — were both shattering in the light of our homeland's erstwhile immunity from foreign attack and morally upsetting in the light of current views on the heinousness of attacking the unarmed and the defenceless. One's close companions were soon contemplating enlistment.

The early absence of two of these I felt very much. Peter Graham joined up early in 1915. It was he who, as assistant at the Natural History Museum in South Kensington had initiated me in beetle hunting, at which he had become quite expert. But the museum's pay was low and he was tempted — unwisely as I thought at the time — to become a menial at the famous Boodles Club, where the money to be obtained in the form of tips was high. A Scotsman on his father's side, he joined a London Territorial battalion and was to see active service, first in Dublin during the Easter Rebellion of 1916, and later in the Middle East, followed by a period on the Western Front in the last months of the war. He survived the perils of the various fronts. Because of poor employment prospects after the war, he re-enlisted, served in peacetime in several overseas stations, and had risen to the rank of sergeant-major in the West Kent Regiment at the time of Dunkirk in 1940, following which, due to the exigencies of the Second World War, I lost touch with him.

The other early recruit, my long-standing school chum, Eddie Collins, and brother of the girl for whom I had an idyllic but inarticulate passion, joined up later in 1915 although still much under age. Son of an impressive Irish footman in the Royal Household, Eddie, an activist rather than an intellectual, was ambitious and meant to do things in life. He joined the Royal Garrison Artillery and had become a bombardier by the time his battery went to Flanders early in 1917, where he was killed within a few months when a chance gas shell registered a direct hit on his dugout.

We were surprised one day during the same eventful year when my father came home with the announcement that he had been accepted for the 2nd Sportsmen's Battalion of the Royal Fusiliers, which was being recruited at the Hotel Cecil in the Strand. We had chipped him once or twice on enlistment, as was the manner of the times, not seriously of course since he was already well into his forties and his health always uncertain. Only a few units were open at the time to men of his age, and we felt that he must have talked his way in, for he had a very plausible way with him, to strangers at least. He always claimed that he had enlisted to save me from going when my time came, which of course was an irrelevance, presumably to excuse himself in my mother's eyes.

The marching and exercises quickly discovered his congenital stomach weakness and he was soon put on tradesman's jobs in the pioneer section, of the sort that the newly constructed army camps especially needed. He was, for example, a good hand at sign-writing, which he had learned from his father, last in a declining line of house builders and decorators in Reading in the latter years of the nineteenth century. Notice-boards were a priority requirement both in camps and in the trenches. My father carried on and was not to be invalided out until 1918, after serving with his regiment at Romford, Leamington, Clipstone and Dover — the latter town at that time being the nearest place in Britain to the front line and the only one subject to land bombardment. He ended up with a spell of several months in the Military Hospital in Mitcham. After the war he was always proud to wear his silver badge, with GRI and Crown and inscribed 'For King and Country — Services Rendered', given to disabled members of the Forces.

I had no personal urge to go until I was wanted, which meant when I reached the enlistment age as determined by the military authorities. Nor did outside pressures amount to much in my case. My health was good of course. It had to be for me to achieve a permanent position in the Civil Service, as I had done before the end of 1914, but I was not a robust-looking type. Working in London one could not avoid becoming to some extent involved in the recruiting drive which continued impressively right up to 1916. The Strand area, in particular, where my new office was situated was literally alive with highly articulate and forceful recruiting sergeants. From the early days it had been a repeatedly amusing sight to see companies of recruits marching through town wearing military top-coats over their civilian suits. I could not have looked my age, for I remember only once being accosted by one of the recruiting terrors, and never did I receive a white feather, which some of the ladies in the early stages of the war thought fit to hand out to other women's men. But the situation did change continuously and rapidly, and before the end of 1915 the authorities were having to face the prospect of the breakdown of the voluntary system of recruitment, which I always ardently supported on principle.

In order to save the situation the Government introduced the Derby scheme of forward recruitment, so called after the name of the Director-General of Recruitment, the Earl of Derby. All fit men between the ages of 18 and 41 were invited to volunteer for call up as and when required. For this purpose they were to be classified in age groups and married or single status, preference for call up being given first to single men according to age, the younger groups being called up first. Volunteers under the scheme were to be enlisted for one day and then deferred until their group was called. The embargo on the enlistment of Civil Servants which had been imposed after the high initial outflow was lifted, and Post Office employees in particular were encouraged to take part in the scheme.

By this time the atmosphere at the office was becoming more and more frustrating. Many had gone before the imposition of the embargo and others were going for special reasons. There had been a steady inflow of women to fill the vacancies on a temporary basis, mostly young women from middle-class families, who were eager enough for the work, but lacking office experience usually had a good deal to learn. The departure of friends outside the office had already helped to dislocate one's private life and altogether the future was unsettled. It was becoming clearer that the war would last long enough to entail one's own participation and that there were therefore good reasons to get the matter settled one way or another.

Consequently on 10th December 1915 I went along to the recruitment office at Scotland Yard, which was dealing with civil servants, attested, took the oath of allegiance, and received a day's pay together with subsistence (amounting, if my memory serves me, to about 3s 4d). I was assigned to Group 1 and placed on reserve until called. I was issued with a khaki armlet emblazoned with the royal crown which, worn on the sleeve announced to the public one's special status and placed one outside the attentions of the recruiting sergeant, who still found plenty to do, for in fact the Derby scheme was only moderately successful, and there were those who still held back and might be winkled out by that sort of persuasion. The Government were soon compelled to introduce conscription, for the unprecedented demands of this new type of war exceeded what the voluntary principle was yielding.

The acquirement of the new status had a subtle psychological effect on me. My views on the war and of becoming a soldier were not altered, but I was now inside the fighting machine and any satisfaction that I still derived from being a civil servant of the Crown was diminished, and a growing uncertainty about the date of my call up (which at the outset did not appear likely before 4th August 1916) added fuel to my undefined discontent. Obviously the job of finishing the war had a special priority to one who had been accepted as an active participant, and I was not sorry when I received notice to report at Wandsworth Town Hall on 3rd May 1916, just three months ahead of my nineteenth birthday.

During the intervening months I had twice attempted to regain an element of initiative by enlisting in a unit of my own choice. I had applied at the depots of both the Honourable Artillery Company and the Civil Service Rifles, but neither of these regiments, who were in a position to be choosey at any time, were much interested in taking someone who was already in the net. It would have complicated the bureaucratic processes already in train. However, I did make a last moment effort in this direction at the Drill Hall of the East Surrey Regiment in Wimbledon, where the Officer Commanding the Administrative Centre was unusually sympathetic and gave me a memorandum to hand to the Recruiting Officer, stating 'I am prepared to accept him if his enlistment for the regiment can be arranged'. But on the day, not a little intimidated by the unbending routine at the recruitment depot at Wandsworth, I decided not to attempt to break the already determined bureaucratic chain. It might not have been any use in any case, for the system was very hidebound, taking little care to meet the wishes of the individual, especially if he was already committed and there was nothing to be gained from bending the routine. Had I successfully done so there can be little doubt that my life would have been differently routed, for I should probably have missed my experiences on the Western Front. I heard subsequently that the particular battalion to which recruits at Wimbledon were being sent at the time was destined for India and the Far East.

Thus it was that on the morning of 3rd May 1916 I said my last farewells to my mother, sister and home and made my way to the mobilisation centre at Wandsworth Town Hall, to join some 150 others of various conditions and ages. The ensuing process was slow: forms had to be made out under the supervision of the army staff, and numerous questions to be answered. At last, after some tedious waits, the whole crowd of us was marshalled outside the Town Hall and marched under the charge of a sergeant to the railway station to entrain for Kingston for further treatment. Marching through the town with my motley companions in very unmilitary formation, despite the sergeant's most earnest efforts, I felt that the doors of civil life were really closing behind me, a feeling to be greatly heightened when we marched through the gates of Kingston barracks into the courtyard, where squads of earlier recruits were being drilled, and orderlies were crossing purposefully at brisk paces in many directions.

In a large hut curtained down the middle our names were called against the roll and we were instructed to prepare for medical examination, a routine with which we would become very familiar in the immediate future. I gathered that we were expected to strip and did not relish this at all. This was the first great ordeal of army life. The enclosure soon became heated and the atmosphere nauseous. The language was unprintable. As their names were called, the men advanced to the curtain and, divesting themselves of their remaining garments, hurried unceremoniously into the unknown. The stream was measured but continuous and shortly its constituents began to emerge from behind the far end of the screen. Their remarks were varied and usually vague. One thought he was all right and hoped not; another thought he had not passed and was sorry since this was his fourth time. All agreed that the testing was severe; the army could still afford to demand reasonably high standards. The country was still filled with fine soldiers in training.

My turn approached and my knees were shaking. It was not the idea of becoming a soldier that caused this intensified fear, but the immediate need to appear naked before strangers. My name was called: I took off my overcoat which was acting as dressing gown and hurried into the chamber of terror. There were four doctors at different tables set apart, each dealing with specific parts of the anatomy. The first looked at my teeth, took my height, weight, and asked one or two questions, the answers being entered upon a form. The papers then passed to the table of the next doctor where my sight was tested against a card of letters attached to the nearby wall.

So far all seemed satisfactory, but I approached the third doctor with no increased confidence for I had noted that he was ordering the men about in a most peremptory manner. He made me skip and jump, and get into ludicrous postures while his pen worked down the form: all this presumably to test agility. The last doctor put his stethoscope to my chest and here a note of doubt entered. It seemed that my chest expansion was below the required standard and the doctor, a more amiable type than the others, was clearly undecided. Upon remarking that I was still under nineteen he suggested that I might be put back a few months. I must have looked disappointed, as indeed I was, for, strange to say, at the moment that was how I felt. I had left the office with something of the halo of the departing hero. Everyone had been kind, and many had promised to write. I could not face the anti-climax of repeating all that. Yet in the light of the developments of the next few months there can be little doubt that even such a short delay would materially have affected my future story.

Anyway, the doctor, noting my reaction, endorsed the papers carefully, and I was ushered into the dressing-room. I cannot say that I was altogether surprised at the doctor's reaction for, despite excellent health since childhood, when I had passed through a pretty testing stage, I had the physique of a clerk rather than of a manual worker. Evidently I had reserves of whose existence even I was unaware: I was to fill out later. I dressed quickly and anxiously awaited the verdict.

Shortly after the last man had reappeared the sergeant entered with a batch of papers and began to read out the names. I had been passed for home service only, and was glad to have the matter settled. Those of us who had been accepted were then conducted to a wing of the barracks to an upstairs chamber where at a trestle table stretching from end to end of the long room, we were served with our first typical army meal of bully beef and hard biscuits, swilled down with a bowl of thick tea. The meal was an uproarious one, most of the men being in high spirits. I had not eaten since breakfast and the unappetising food went down quite well; the biscuit certainly was hard but the bully beef quite palatable. Then came the welcome news of the day. Accommodation in the barracks being limited, those of us who wished could go home for the night on the strict understanding that we reported back by 9 a.m. sharp the following morning. Then we were reminded that we were soldiers now and warned ominously that those who did not report to time would be counted as deserters and dealt with accordingly.

After an excited return home to report upon the happenings of the day and enjoy one further night in my own bed, I returned to barracks in due time and learned that I had been assigned to the Hertfordshire Regiment. As this seemed a good enough choice I was not sorry that, taking the line of least resistance, I had not brought out my conditional acceptance for the East Surreys. Those recruits who had passed for active service were being assigned to the West Kents. I was glad to have missed the particular battalion, which, we were told by those in the know at the barracks, were a pretty rough lot. Of all those who had reported the morning before only about a third had been passed and of these about a dozen had been accepted for home service only.

Under the charge of a beribboned old soldier with the rank of lance-corporal we were marshalled to Hertford via Kings Cross. It felt very strange being thus escorted from station to station, including two changes on the underground railway, under military control, and I was not a little pleased with myself although still dressed in 'civvies'. My companions were inclined to be rowdy in the train. They did not strike me as being any more favourable military material than myself, some in fact having obvious disabilities and, not surprisingly, a record of numerous earlier rejections. Their language disgusted my middle-class sensitivity. This, I knew, I should have to get used to, as, indeed I soon did for it was all so repetitive that it soon lost its impact and any point it may have had.

We reached the pleasant little country town of Hertford at midday, and I was assigned with three others to a private billet on the far side of the town, away from the railway station. The people of the billet were kind and homely, and obviously well used to looking after recruits who normally stayed for a few days before going to join the battalion. The food was wholesome and plentiful and not, as I rightly surmised, a fair sample of the army diet we should have to endure. I was assigned to a small cosy room of my own, which delighted me, looking out upon green countryside crossed in the middle distance by a row of tall elms, which stays in my memory as the shelter of a considerable colony of very voluble rooks. Among my companions in the billet was one named Richards, a city clerk, a quiet intelligent man some years my senior, and another named King, a countryman with open healthy countenance, a slow thinker with abundant kindness of heart. I regarded myself as fortunate in their company.

The regimental depot of our distinguished territorial regiment consisted of a group of small buildings surrounded by a miniature parade ground, situated some few hundred yards below the billet. During that afternoon we were issued with khaki tunic, trousers and puttees, heavy boots and peaked hat. Putting them on for the first time I felt a fearful guy: they were all so new and shapeless, while the boots, though I took only size six at the time, felt as though they were weighted with lead.

During the evening I walked into town with Richards. We looked at the castle, and were astonished to see a shattered house which had been struck in one of the previous year's air raids. On our way back from that stroll we passed an officer and were much put to it to supply the salute which we knew was expected of us but which we had not yet had occasion to practise. However, our effort seemed to pass muster.

On my first morning I awoke to sunshine and the cawing of the rooks which seemed to be greeting the lovely day with excessive vigour. Our hosts took the opportunity to expand at breakfast and I was introduced to the very intelligent son who showed me his neat little stamp collection, and evinced great interest in the countryside. He was on very good terms with one of the depot men, who had the good fortune to be billeted there.

We paraded under the eye of a lance-corporal, an old soldier of modest stature, with bushy moustache and most disagreeable manner, which seemed to be normal in institutions of that sort. We were given basic instruction on army procedure and were exercised in marching, turning, saluting and so forth, and it was surprising how difficult were such simple evolutions, especially in our heavy army boots, though I may have gained just a little advantage from my previous experience with the Kensington Cadet Corps.

During the first afternoon our metamorphosis into military robots was further advanced by the issue of tough army underwear, a kit bag and a puzzle of leather equipment to carry pack, entrenching tool, waterbottle, haversack and ammunition pouches, with which we were also furnished. All this came to us as a medley of separate items, which had to be put together in a set pattern so as to fit closely over the tunic and give us all a similar appearance on parade. It was all so confusing that I felt at the outset I should never get the hang of it, but this was of course a delusion, and in any case we were soon pulled up if we got anything wrong. A strap that crossed left over right could not possibly be allowed to cross right over left.

Our group of some fifty recruits was split into two equal batches, one to join the second battalion at Newmarket and the other the fourth battalion at Thetford. I welcomed being attached to the former, who, we were told, were billeted in stables, rather than the latter who were under canvas. Not that Newmarket sounded an alluring destination, from reports current at the depot. Richards, King and I were assigned to the same unit.

The following day we moved by rail to Newmarket and immediately on our arrival were assigned to our respective companies, we three with two others going to B Company, which was stationed in racing stables on the edge of the town and of the heath, that training ground of many notable racehorses. The men occupied the horse-boxes surrounding a quadrangle. These seemed clean enough, but with their cement walls and stone floors the prospect was very bleak. We were fortunate therefore, since accommodation in the stables was short, to be allocated to private billets some ten minutes walk away. Richards and I were sent to the same billet, which we shared with Day, a drummer who had been with the regiment for some time and knew all the ropes, which was much to our advantage. We rejoiced in having a comfortable bed for a little longer, but wondered how we should manage to be on parade as quickly as the rest of the company.

An early task was to report to the company quarter-master-sergeant — CQMS — for our kit to be checked over and certain missing items to be added — comb, brush, razor, holdall, and that sort of thing. Unlike most of the NCOs so far encountered the CQMS was a very friendly type, and we were not surprised to discover that he was universally liked and a great favourite with the troops. This was quite the normal pattern as far as my experience went: the CQMS needed to be administrator rather than soldier.

We took our meals with the rest in the messroom attached to the stables, sitting at a long trestle table, while the food, brought in large containers was ladled into bowls, which were passed along from hand to hand until everyone was served. It was all very rough and ready, as was to be expected, but the food was wholesome enough and reasonably well cooked. There were meat and vegetable courses and a sweet course. I certainly made a good meal on that first occasion and did not find the surroundings particularly uncongenial, but I was surprised to notice that many of the other recruits, as well as old hands, looked at the food askance and left their plates and bowls half full. This was to be a continuing experience during the training phase and grumbling about the food was prevalent. It surprised me at the time because I was sure that the majority were getting more and probably better cooked food than they could possibly have afforded at home. To me it seemed there was plenty to get worked up about without exaggerating details of that sort. The recruits had a table of their own in the corner of the mess and a real mixture we were, many coming from the London slums. It was the blueness of the language that upset me most. I had to learn.

That evening I accompanied Richards on an exploration of the town, a sleepy sort of place consisting mainly of one broad street lined with unpretentious shops, though obviously it was no longer its normal self. The street was crowded with meandering Tommies, among whom the proportion of officers seemed high so that the constant need to salute was a nuisance. One dared not ignore this duty since there were sufficient military police looking for an excuse to pounce upon defaulters at the least omission. We discovered the well-equipped Soldiers' Home, which provided light refreshments at nominal charges, had a reading and writing room with plenty of magazines, also a lecture hall fitted up with a stage. The atmosphere was free and pleasant enough and the home would offer a haven while we remained in Newmarket. Both Richards and I were shocked by conditions in the streets, which besides the teeming soldiers were filled with parading girls and women, some arm in arm with men, others standing on the sidelines smirking at every uniformed male who passed. I returned to billet quite depressed.

The following day being Sunday, we got up in a leisurely way, since our only assignment was to attend Church parade, for which there was ample time. But we had much to learn about the army and were soon disabused of the notion that we could ever count upon being left alone. Immediately after breakfast we were instructed to prepare for medical inspection. The recruits and trained men were to parade separately. The latter consisted mainly of those members of the original battalion who had not been sent to France with the first line or subsequent drafts. Recently the drafting had stopped and the battalion was now designated only for home service.

We assembled outside the stables for the inspection and waited about stripped to the waist for our turn to enter. Inside, the Medical Officer and our Company Commander sat at a table. There everything was brisk and perfunctory. A sharp word of command from the sergeant-major, and I stepped forward.

'Name?'

'Gladden.'

'Any complaints?'

'No, Sir.'

A superficial scrutiny by the M.O., who was apparently checking my appearance with the papers on the table in front of him, and I was dismissed. Some of the others were questioned in more detail, and tapped here and there by the M.O., who might also use his stethoscope, but by and large the whole business seemed little more than a routine and could have served little medical purpose.

Within a matter of days my medical rating was raised to A II, which meant fit for active service after training.

On the following Friday I took part in my first pay parade, a ceremony to a set pattern to which I should become well accustomed during the next few years. Each man walked smartly up to the pay table to salute and receive his wage from the paying officer and to acknowledge this with a further salute. All this took place under the eagle-eye of the sergeant-major, who compered the whole operation as if heaven and earth depended upon it. As a single man, making no allowances, I received a total of 6s 6d (which was a good enough sum for pocket-money at that time).

On our second Sunday we did in fact attend church parade, equipped only with belt and bayonet and being marched to the church. The Roman Catholics and the Methodists and Wesleyans were called out separately and marched away, each to their own place of worship, while the rest of us were treated as Church of England. I've no doubt that on occasions some of the latter did opt out on the grounds that they were not members of the Church, but it was easier not to and I do not personally recollect this happening. During the afternoon Richards, King and I walked out into the countryside, at our doorstep, then bright with spring foliage, and were pleased to be free for a while from all army routine, which is oppressive even when nothing much is expected of one. Even on such jaunts it was necessary to be properly groomed, with buttons brightly burnished, wearing a well-polished belt and carrying an army cane embellished with the regimental crest (in our case featuring a stag) and purchasable in the shops.

By the middle of the month I was getting used to the daily parades, which ran to a routine and were generally boring. We had been issued with long-muzzled Lee-Enfield rifles, and were being instructed in their handling. For 16th May I set down our day's routine in detail. It was a fair example of how we passed our time and would continue so to do, except when special events intervened. Moreover it was the sort of pattern that operated in the army during the war, even on active service.

5.45 a.m. reveille. We usually heard the bugle call, but if not Day came in without fail to rout us out. Speed was essential as there was much cleaning up to do before the parade.

7.00 a.m. we fell in at the stables in shirt sleeves and without puttees, for physical jerks under the Physical Training Sergeant, who took us all, officers included, at a quick pace out on to the heath where we spent the next forty minutes marching, running and at various physical exercises. The P.T. Sergeant, named Smith, was an ex-policeman, a big fellow with a short temper and extremely caustic wit. He successfully raised a good deal of mirth, especially from among those who wanted to keep in his good books and stay at the depot. As soon as we were dismissed we quickly put on our puttees, an art which some were slow in acquiring, and tunics and assembled for breakfast, which was scheduled for 8 a.m. Although this was our first meal, the men in the stables had already enjoyed, on rising, tea as 'gunfire'.

8.40 a.m. we paraded in the quadrangle under our respective sergeants, again in groups of trained men and recruits separately, according to the orders posted the night before setting out the day's programme.

It happened that our NCO, a Sergeant Thompson, was a very pleasant chap, and hearing the others at their raucous work, we counted ourselves particularly fortunate. His first task was to draw us up into line, cover us off, call the roll and then inspect our equipment and general appearance in order to put things right before the officers came on parade. The Company-Sergeant-Major, a stumpy old soldier of severe demeanour, then took particulars of those present, and we awaited the arrival of the Company Commander, Captain Palmer.

9.00 a.m. the officers then came on parade and carried out an even more severe inspection, any faults being loudly announced to all and sundry in a manner that caused even the most hardboiled to tremble. Our Captain, an ex-Guards officer who had already served at the front, was greatly respected by his company. He was, as might have been expected, a stickler for discipline, but of easy manner when off parade. He had acquired the knack of getting the best out of his men. One knew at once when he was on parade and it need hardly be said that the old hands, who knew a good deal about his career, held him in high esteem. For the next three hours we were drilled in numerous exercises, marching, handling arms, and so forth, successively by the sergeants and officers but only occasionally as a company by the Captain. After three hours of this gruelling 'mucking about', as we irreverently called it, we were dismissed for the dinner break.

Now intervened a very popular occasion. At about 12.30 the Company Postman, usually a lance-corporal, brought in the mail. We crowded round him, prepared to call out loudly whenever our own names were called. It was one of a soldier's greatest pleasures to receive letters from home and friends. Some were fortunate and received a numerous mail, while others rarely heard their names called. I was always in the more fortunate majority. One studious-looking private named Brown, with the initials E.R., was in this category and the cause of a daily ritual in which we all participated every time his name was called, by shouting uproariously 'Ere y'ar Brown'.

1.00 p.m. the midday meal was served in the messroom. The food was ample and not at all bad, although there were the usual grumbles from those who did not like this or that. I had discovered that being spoilt was not confined to the children of the well-to-do. Sometimes the Orderly Officer came round and the Orderly Sergeant, who accompanied him, called for complaints, but this had become a mere routine since there never were any.

1.50 to 4.00 p.m. the parades continued according to plan, although in the afternoon the proceedings were usually less strenuous, consisting generally of verbal instruction about the rifle, or more general talks. Some of the topics, such as range-finding, I found particularly interesting, preferring this sort of thing to the repetitive marching, wheeling and so forth. For this purpose we sat round in groups, often on the grass away from the buildings. The sergeant, taking the particular topic, explained the art of judging distance in relation to particular objects, placing members of the group at specific intervals to demonstrate relative visibility.

The majority of the recruits seemed rather thick-headed, needing to make a considerable mental effort to learn any new exercise or to acquire facts outside their normal experience. I found little difficulty, even with the manual exercises and manipulations in which I had little interest. I recognized that, despite my basically unmilitary nature, I was able to carry out the programme to the letter without undue strain upon nerves or muscles.

Sergeant Thompson demonstrated his unusual friendliness by breaking off from time to time to chat about the old battalion, which had a great peacetime reputation in the Territorial Army and to which the old hands owed a great loyalty. He passed on news from the front, as conveyed in letters and reports from friends serving in the line, and his remarks ranged over the war in its wider sense and in particular upon the prospects of our personal participation in the battle line before it finished. In his opinion we stood a good chance of going overseas eventually, but not into the firing line in view of our general unfitness. I had doubts about this, for we all at the time hoped and half expected that the war would be over in 1916.

5.00 p.m. tea was served: tea, bread and butter and jam. The evenings were free unless there was some special exercise.

I found my companions amiable enough, but their incessant coarse language monotonous. Although it was difficult to take seriously the details of the nightly amours as recounted at the mess table with gusto and without reticence, visual evidence in the streets in the evening did lend a good deal of support to the Rabelaisian stories. One of these romancers stands out in my memory. Although still young he had a seamed and rugged face, in some ways the ugliest I had ever seen, yet there was an extraordinary gentleness in his manner and disposition, characteristics that made him a universal favourite in the company. If only a fraction of his nocturnal reports were true he had the mythical Don Juan beaten to a frazzle.

Richards and I had much more modest ambitions. A typical evening was spent on a trip along the High Street to make some purchases, which in my case may have been a novel, perhaps a work of H.G. Wells to whom I was addicted, or of Charles Garvice whose love stories were all the rage at the time and widely available. In any case my literary taste was not then very discriminating. The rest of our time was probably spent in the Soldiers' Home, writing letters and reading the day's papers. On one occasion we played chess, at which I was no adept, though it is possible that I had potentialities which I never found the time to develop. Richards, who obviously fancied himself at the game and had expected easy victory, seemed annoyed that I managed to win rather more games than he did. Refreshments at the Soldiers' Home were very cheap: for example, a cup of tea, coffee or cocoa cost a halfpenny. Our supper amounted to a penny or twopence.

On 17th May we were fortunate to have the afternoon free and be able to go out on the heath to witness the New Derby, which was being run under wartime conditions at Newmarket instead of Epsom. In this way the authorities were doing their best to keep the flag of horse-racing flying. But the scene was very different from its peacetime version, which I had once had the good fortune to attend, in horse and trap, with my parents. The crowd now were mainly in khaki and all the picturesque touches of the Epsom event were lacking. Unless one was well-informed about horses and personally interested in them, which I certainly was not, the racing itself offered little to enthuse over, unless one was involved in the betting. On this occasion Richards and I were accompanied by a rather older member of our company, a man in his thirties named Collet, who most certainly was interested in horses and able to convey something of his involvement and understanding to others. Collet was a sympathetic person to whom the army was an unrewarding duty. (He was to remain on home service and to continue to correspond with me after I left the regiment.) It was evident from the manner of some members of the crowd that there were touts present on the course and soldiers trying to make bets, but this was clearly frowned upon by the military police who were present in force.

Our afternoon off was to be counterbalanced by our first experience of night operations, as they were called, which were scheduled from 8.30 to 10.30 p.m. that evening. This was a sufficiently mild affair, calculated to get us used to taking orders and moving about with discipline and silently in the dark. All we did in fact was march across the heath and then skirmish back in open order through the dusk towards the town; an activity which seemed aimed more at sorting out the officers than the rank and file.

On Saturdays we followed the half-day custom of completing parades at noon. For an hour on the morning of 20th May we were treated to one of those army occasions that worked out very much to pattern. The whole unit was drawn up in companies for battalion drill. Normally our drilling went on in company under the Captain or in platoon under one of the Second Lieutenants, and we soon got used to these evolutions. Battalion drills were another matter, a much more complicated and less rehearsed process which tended to run into difficulties. The four companies were drawn up on the heath, with the Regimental Sergeant Major and the Adjutant to the fore, the Colonel giving the commands, and the company, platoon, and section leaders taking up the running in sequence, as the individual evolutions required. It was hardly a matter for surprise that, with our lack of experience, the attempts to form line on the march, to divide off into companies and so forth, soon had chaotic consequences, and our leaders' tempers were badly frayed. This gave great scope to the fault-finding propensities of the NCOs, eager to cover up their own confusions. Whenever an officer shouted his dissatisfaction with platoon or company, all the NCOs in the vicinity began rushing back and forth like a pack of yapping dogs, cursing everyone within reach, thus adding to the pandemonium without helping in the least to sort out the muddle. At length the Colonel, having obviously had enough, handed the parade over to the Regimental Sergeant Major and we prepared for real trouble. His solution was to draw us up into line and to test our proficiency in arms drill. Considering the large recruit element on parade, I felt that we came through this ordeal much better than could have been expected — tribute to our task-master of the moment. We were not without casualties, however, and some who perpetrated easily observable mistakes

— for the more agile found little difficulty in covering up in such a large assemblage — were given a dressing down in a voice charged with sarcasm and at such a pitch as to be heard, I felt certain, in Newmarket itself.

The parade ended in time for our weekly medical inspection, which was carried out behind the 'D' Company billets, where we stood, tunics off, shirts open at the neck, sleeves rolled up, and waited. The M.O. walked slowly along the lines, accompanied by the Captain, whose demeanour clearly implied that this was hardly his cup of tea. The MO reprimanded one or two for not being clean, but in the main the whole occasion seemed very much a matter of routine. I was told that the main object of these inspections was to spot skin diseases, such as scabies, which were then pretty widespread. As my chest was habitually covered with a light rash at that time I was apprehensive about this, but the MO passed on without comment, and I breathed again.

Now followed another of the army's common parades, namely kit inspection, carried out on this occasion by Captain Palmer. Those of us who were in billets had to carry our kits to the stables. The groundsheet, which we all had, provided a satisfactory container in which to convey the rest of our belongings. These had then to be arranged on the groundsheet to a pattern, strictly according to regulations, designed to render it possible for the checking to be done almost at a glance. Each in turn was interrogated on deficiencies and cautioned both upon unexplained gaps and upon incorrect procedures. The CQMS made a note of each mam's deficiencies and we then packed up for the day.

During the following week I had my first experience of a route march, which I actually enjoyed and was always to prefer to the normal parade. On this occasion the entire battalion took to the road, following the pleasant route through the villages of Moulton and Cheveley. Provided one kept in line — at that time in column of fours — and in step, the discipline of the march was not burdensome, except when the battalion was brought to attention with sloped arms all at the correct angle. Regulations prescribed a five-minute halt in every hour, when with packs off one could relax at the side of the road. We had a drum and fife band, and it was surprising how the regular beat of the big drum helped us along.

We could talk and sing. There was a good deal of singing, led by the trained hands who had a versatile repertory, but we all joined in, so far as we knew the words. Of course, the popular songs were familiar to most of us, but there were army ditties which, sung on the public highway within civilian hearing, I found embarrassing. However, the officers seemed to enjoy them as much as the men. My dislike of verbal coarseness could have been due to my youth, though the fact that I have never overcome that dislike suggests a rooted idiosyncrasy. It is however important in retrospect to take into account my reactions in this matter, which in our later permissive society could well be considered unwarranted or at least exaggerated, since those reactions added to the military burdens that weighed upon such a youngster as I. Others had different foibles.

On 26th May I noted down our menus for the day, which are a fair example of our rations at that time. Our three meals consisted of (1) breakfast: haddock, marmalade, bread and butter; (2) dinner: Irish stew and date pudding; (3) tea: bread, butter, jam and tea. The helpings were simple and often a second portion was to be had. The cooking was satisfactory, but the service left a good deal to be desired. The containers and crockery were only passably clean. Compared with what we were to get later all this was fair enough, although there was a lot of grumbling and most of us were hungry in the evenings, hence the popularity of the Soldiers' Home.

We had a 'conchy' (conscientious objector) in the company, a queer bird to most of us. He was giving the authorities a good deal of trouble, refusing parades and all instructions. He had already managed to get away in civilian clothes and had been brought back under escort. A quiet, well-spoken fellow in his mid-twenties, whose glasses gave him a studious look, I formed the opinion that he was sincere in his views. He was certainly going to considerable trouble in upholding them. He got little support from the company. The boys often gathered round him when he was resting on his bed in the billet, trying to draw him out with questions which he answered readily, refusing to get ruffled. When asked the stock question what he would do if his home was entered by Germans and his mother or sister threatened with rape, he answered that his beliefs did not permit him to meet force with force.

To me his views were misguided, as I believed there was an overriding obligation on every free citizen to protect the nation in the face of foreign aggression. I felt too that a sincere pacifist who would not participate in the taking of life could always volunteer for non-combatant duties, especially in the Royal Army Medical Corps, whose members could not be accused of what we called 'dodging the column'. It must be remembered that the granting of the legal right to opt out to genuine conscientious objectors was a very new idea to us at the time.

That night Zeppelins passed overhead and dropped bombs in the neighbourhood, but I have no personal recollection of what happened since I slept right through the hullabaloo, and the tales at breakfast were no more reliable than the normal reports of such happenings.

Cases of measles were reported in the surrounding camps, and to prevent an epidemic the company was confined to the stables, much to the men's chagrin. Those of us who were in billets evaded the ban as it was easy to explain our way past the pickets.

On the last day of May, as a welcome change to the ordinary parades, accompanied by the field kitchens we marched to a place called Dillington Road where the authorities had constructed a model trench system, purporting to convey a realistic idea of the conditions at the front. Our assigned task was to destroy the model and fill in the trenches, and for this purpose picks and shovels were supplied to us. Before undertaking our task we were able to inspect the extensive system of trenches. Speaking from his own experience at the front, the Captain explained the working of the system, the several trench lines, with bays and fire step, dugouts, communication trenches, machine-gun emplacements, company headquarters, and so forth. We became so interested as to regret the need to destroy the handiwork which we were examining. I could not avoid with apprehension imagining how it would be at the real front and wondering what would be my personal reactions with bullets and shells and other enemy action, and did not find myself eager for the experience. There was consolation in the thought that the call would not be for some time yet.

We set to work with pick and shovel but progress was slow for there was more to be done than had at first appeared. At the end of the day the job was little more than half completed. I felt very much a novice in the use of the shovel, and many were the criticisms of the way in which the clerks among us used the tools, from the ex-navvies and labourers who were thoroughly at home with these implements. However, I noticed that many of the manual workers were little more expert with them than the rest of us. The operation was tackled in an unusually egalitarian spirit, officers and NCOs taking turn at the pick and shovelling. We did not carry on past 4.00 p.m. In retrospect it is evident that the task, though necessary, had been undertaken as a part of our training to introduce us to an activity which the conditions of trench warfare made vital for the infantryman.

The first of June was a lovely day and we were fortunate to be scheduled for a march which took us through Moulton to Suicide's Corner and Waterhall Farm. The trees were now thickly clad in vivid greenery and the countryside looking at its best. I welcomed the chance to breathe the clean air and found the experience highly invigorating, a real consolation in the military experience.

Two days later, after the afternoon parade, we received instructions to prepare ourselves for inoculation against typhoid. The idea was distasteful to me and I dreaded the operation. Such feelings were almost universal. Indeed many of the men were resentful and vehement in their protests and swore they would not submit to the indignity. There was an impression that inoculation could be refused on conscientious grounds, but this would have been difficult to support since the injections were aimed to protect the army rather than the individual ranker. They were for the general benefit, a policy that the experience of the War was to justify fully. In the event nothing much happened when the MO went to work.

We were drawn up outside the stables with tunics off, and filed steadily in before the doctor who got on with the job expeditiously. No one was eager for the ordeal. One man fainted in the waiting queue, while a few collapsed afterwards. It should be remarked that much of this was due to the fact that the inoculation was a completely new experience to which we should later become accustomed, when such reaction would be exceptional.

As at the dentist the real strain arose from the waiting. My turn came at last and I felt extremely apprehensive, envying those who had already passed through. Instructing me to pull back my shirt, the orderly painted my left breast with iodine, the smell of which increased my nervousness. I stepped before the MO. Drawing the serum from a tube into a fearsome-looking syringe with a steel needle some inches long, he brandished the weapon above my shoulder and, taking the loose flesh of my chest between his forefinger and thumb, jabbed it quickly and deeply. The instant pain was followed by an indescribable sickly sensation as the point scraped a rib bone — and the job was done. With heartfelt relief I left the stables and donned my tunic. Of immediate effect there was nothing other than a slight soreness from the puncture. We were to be allowed forty-eight hours without duty, which promised ample consolation.

Both Richards and I went to bed early feeling very hot and sweating profusely. We were without doubt in the grip of fever, and my head was swimming. I dropped off to sleep quickly and was pleased when I awoke early the next morning to discover that the effects were moderating. I was amused to hear Richards talking deliriously in his sleep. He was quite upset about this when I mentioned it in the morning, although his ravings had not made sense.

As it turned out we were both fortunate and were now able really to enjoy our 'vacation'. Having been advised that exercise would be good to increase the effectiveness of the inoculation, we went for a long walk across the heath enjoying the bright summer sunshine. And that was all it did to us. On the other hand some of the men in the stables were really ill and stayed in bed most of the time looking half dead. I could not assess how much of the illness was genuine and how much due to sheer nerves or indeed simulated as an act of protest. Suffice it to say that those who took it badly had nothing to show for their sufferings for they had to be back on duty with the rest of us.

On the night of 23rd June orders were posted for the battalion to prepare to move without delay. We spent the following day packing our kits, carrying blankets, equipment and stores to the railway station and cleaning the billets. The NCOs were in their element, even the sergeants, usually a little withdrawn, were fussing around, ordering us to pick up the smallest scrap of paper, preliminary to the Captain's inspection to ensure that the billet was left tidy and clean as a new pin. Those of us in private billets had brought our equipment into the messroom in order to be ready for an early departure the following morning.

There was little sleep to be had that night; card-playing went on in the messroom until a late hour, some of the men in fact continuing until reveille. Some passed the time singing popular songs, mostly of the pathetic sentimental sort, such as 'I Want to Go Back to the Farm', as well as the usual army ditties, some of which were really coarse. Those of us who remember those times can fairly interpret the present permissive society as having done little more than bring into the open human proclivities which had always been manifested in the habits and attitudes of a large sector of society, not necessarily confined to the so-called lower orders.

At 2.30 a.m. reveille was sounded and instructions shouted for us to get immediately ready to move. We were soon sleepily adjusting our equipment and packs in the shadowy light of the few flares outside the stables. Weird shadows danced among the ranks as the sergeants called the rolls to assure themselves their flocks were all present. After a good deal of messing about in normal army style, we marched to the railway station and entrained for our new billets. Fortunately we were not crowded and were able to make ourselves sufficiently comfortable in the far from comfortable third-class carriages of the period to enable us to make up for some of our lost sleep during the six-hour journey to the north. The massive cathedrals of Ely, Lincoln and York, visible from the train, distinguished the route as we journeyed towards our destination, Harrogate, which we reached at 3.30 p.m.

Parading outside the station, a good deal of time was wasted before we set off along a tedious four-mile march to the camp on Killinghall Moor. Was this spot selected because of the prophetic element in its title? The flat expanse of moorland was covered with tents and marquees in various stages of completion. Reaching the section assigned to our unit we were immediately detailed to bell tents, in groups of nine or ten including the NCO or old soldier chosen to take charge. I regarded myself fortunate to belong to a group of only nine.

The tents were supplied with boarded floors which raised us from direct contact with the ground, a desirable arrangement that was not always to be provided in future camps. Working in accordance with the advice of those who had had previous experience, we spent some time in digging a drainage trench round the tent under the guy ropes as a precaution in case of rain. The surrounding countryside appeared bleak though certainly not unpleasing. I had already been struck on the way up by the replacement of hedges by granite walls dividing the fields, a characteristic of the northern landscape that was new to me. I retrieved my kitbag from the dump and received two blankets for my bed. We seemed rather crowded, although in fact a bell-tent would hold more and in cold weather there was real advantage in being wedged tightly — heads to canvas, feet to the centre pole — provided there were not too many restless souls who wanted to turn frequently.

I awoke the following morning none the worse for my night under canvas and concluded that my somewhat fearful anticipations had been largely imaginary. We took a poor view of the instruction, issued immediately after rising, that blankets should be folded in a regulation manner and stacked outside the tent, covered by a waterproof as protection from the damp. All equipment had also to be cleared out of the tent which had to be opened up. We foresaw trouble should the weather change. The drainage of the camp was defective, the water supply was inadequate, and the sanitary arrangements for so many men were primitive.

Harrogate had been placed out of bounds to the troops. It was common knowledge that some of the townsfolk, on learning of the advent of army units to the area for training, had moved heaven and earth to have them excluded from the town entirely, but such an unpatriotic policy had not been allowed to succeed, although restrictions had been imposed. We were not very pleased by what we heard, but naturally such a handsome, finely planned town in lovely surroundings was to prove an irresistible attraction to dwellers in a badly serviced, half-constructed camp out on the moors, so the demand for passes was heavy, an additional job for the company clerk. It is possible that the attitude of the local authorities had some influence in conditioning the military authorities in bearing the extra work and making it easy for us to enjoy such visits, for in practice there was little difficulty in obtaining a pass.

Consequently I was able to visit Harrogate on our first evening and was impressed by the town in which, in later years, I was to spend some months. The shops were a boon and well stocked compared with those in Newmarket. I soon discovered that the evening 'monkey parade', as it came to be called, of the two sexes in the main streets was little different from what I had already encountered, and I realized there was some reason for the townsfolk's apprehensions.

A couple of days later, reveille being at the unearthly hour of 5.00 a.m., we paraded at 6.45 to go in groups to wash in the Oak Beck, a prettily situated stream not far from camp — an effort to remedy the lack of facilities in the camp. The only other parade that day was a route march, leaving us free, after the midday meal in the company mess-tent. A group of us decided to return to the beck for a swim. The sun was shining brightly, making the waters, though shaded by the trees fringing the stream, appear warm and inviting. Although never more than a mediocre swimmer I had early acquired the habit of not dallying on the brink but diving in head first with the least delay, to avoid the suspense and trepidation, with which so many face the water. On this occasion I decided, for discretion in a strange pool, to omit the header and to jump in. The water of the beck was ice cold and I was immediately overwhelmed and floundered breathlessly to the surface. I scrambled up the bank with little dignity. Most of my companions wisely decided to leave well alone and were content to tarry in a delightful spot out of touch with the tensions of camp.

On the fateful 1st July, when the great Somme offensive

opened in France, there was nothing out of the usual on Killinghall Moor to indicate that an event of shattering importance to all of us, even to many then unborn, was in progress across the Channel. The day had a special significance to me because my name was posted for fire picket. This duty entailed a good deal of effort between the normal drills, in cleaning rifle and polishing equipment, to satisfy the inspection with which the day's picket was inaugurated. Certainly a high level of spotlessness and shine were prescribed for such quasi-ceremonial occasions, but our actual achievement was not good enough to satisfy the junior officer in charge, who excelled himself in fault-finding and in futile attempts to assess the relative brilliancy of our brass buttons and buckles and the consistency in shade of our polished leather equipment. Beyond this we were merely admonished to stand by in case of fire in the camp, and that was that.

During these early days at the camp our rations had become meagre, particularly for dinner. On one occasion when the orderly sergeant had shouted the usual 'Any complaints?', one of the men actually stood up and complained about the smallness of his portion of meat, which was a fairly representative one.

There was no follow through. The officer merely looked at the plate, remarked somewhat superciliously, 'I've had worse than that myself', and passed on. We certainly admired that private for his pluck.

It took some days for the happenings in France to percolate into our consciousness. The initial announcements of great victories were only gradually modified by a realisation that the great push had produced meagre results when measured on the war maps and that the expected break-through had failed to be realised, so far at any rate. The pattern already seemed to be similar to previous offensives, except that this one had been organized on a scale so far unknown in the history of warfare. The terrible price in lives was not to become clear for some time.

At this period we were suffering from rain which lasted almost continuously for seven days, and no worse place could be imagined for such a climatic onslaught than the Yorkshire moors. The camp, already poorly drained, became a quagmire, the mud seeping into the tents and permeating everything. Keeping our rifles and equipment clean became a major task and the parades, scheduled to a close training programme, had to be undertaken between downpours. We did not, of course, realise it at the time but, for some of us at least, this period of dire discomfort was a mere curtain raiser to the much worse experience that was in store.

With a welcome return to fine weather, the company was subjected to a spell of road-making on a new route through the camp. This entailed the breaking of stones and spreading them to form an effective surface. It was hard, monotonous work, with little profit, as far as I could judge at the time. One evening I went to the YMCA tent for an excellent concert organized by members of the Northamptonshire Regiment, the sort of entertainment that was getting under way to improve life in the camp. One day a group of us, armed with axes and saws, were detailed under a corporal to proceed to woods in the vicinity to chop wood for the kitchens. We took our rations for the day and this was a pleasant respite from drills, spent in charming scenery. Having collected sufficient logs to replenish the battalion store, we loaded them on a trolley which we manhandled back to camp.

At this time, in the horse lines of a Yeomanry regiment situated in the rear of our camp, we witnessed a sight which caused both anger and dismay in our ranks, as well as pity for the victim whatever his fault may have been. One of the rankers had obviously been convicted of a serious offence against army regulations and sentenced to march up and down for long spells carrying his full pack, blanket and rifle and to be continuously chivvied by the raucous commands of an unsympathetic drill sergeant.

Armed with a week-end pass — which was necessary to proceed beyond camp limits — and a free railway warrant, I went off the following week-end on my first leave to London; a great joy to me, if all too short. On my way back I had time, when I changed trains at Holbeck, to have a look round. Habituated to the much more amiable residential streets around Earl's Court and my new home at Putney, I was shocked by this Yorkshire industrial area, which was not merely down at heel and drab but literally dirty, as though the inhabitants were without self-respect. Even here there were other elements of a pseudo-romantic nature, although this did not appear from a cursory contact with the ill-dressed people I passed in the streets or saw chatting on doorsteps. The brief halt had not been too short for some of the soldiers returning from leave — if their word was to be accepted — to find both the time and opportunity 'to get off', as they called it.

At this time an opportunity arose for me to volunteer to take a Lewis-gun course which I welcomed as a release from the monotony of the ordinary parades. In fact, although I was not much interested in things mechanical I found the lectures and detailed instruction interesting, though this assignment was to prove no more than a flash in the pan.

By now life in camp was much better organized and I was finding conditions reasonably bearable. We had been unfortunate as a unit to be in at the beginning, for it takes time to build up the type of amenities that such a camp needs. The weather too had improved.

Crowding in the tent was always irksome to me, although in the main our particular group were an amiable lot. My views differed radically from those of the majority and I often found myself in a minority of one. I do not remember what were then the main bones of contention, but have no doubt that I took exception to their philosophy on matters of sex, which I regarded with the ideals of a young romantic. This was not really surprising for most of my companions were older than me. No doubt I was foolish to take their attitudes on these and certain other matters too much to heart, but I was of a religious temperament, held idealist views on the mission of humanity, and was not much inclined to be forgiving to those who fell by the wayside.

Apart from Richards, who had now been transferred to another part of the camp with the prospect of a stripe in view, there were three of my colleagues with whom I had become particularly friendly, all of whom took much the same view as I did on military life. They were Bratley, whose image is among those that have become faded, the somewhat older Collet, lover of horses, and Jimmy Downs. The last had become a close friend and we were destined to be, in army parlance, sparring partners, or pals. He was a quietly spoken, sincere young man, perhaps a year or two older than me. A devout Roman Catholic and unmarried, he had been brought up by two devoted maiden aunts who lived in Bromley, Kent. From what he told me about these dear 'old' ladies they must have been devastated when their beloved nephew had gone off to the wars. Their charge did them great credit.

My probings into the charms of the Yorkshire countryside continued during our off moments. One fine evening, armed with the pass that was necessary if one was to walk boldly past the pickets one might meet on the road, I took the train to Knaresborough. I travelled alone since I had been unable to find anyone on this occasion keen on this sort of jaunt. The urge to reach the next village, to see beyond the next hill, had always been a characteristic of mine, a characteristic that had received early encouragement from ownership of a bicycle and addiction to the open road. Knaresborough, with its lovely setting, historic castle and pleasant thoroughfares was — and no doubt still is — a fascinating place. For this, my first visit, I armed myself, at the modest cost of one penny, with a copy of the nineteenth edition of the *Official Handbook and Illustrated Guide*, published in 1915.

After church parade on 30th July, a wave of excitement swept the camp when urgent orders were issued for us to stand-by. All stores were packed, the kitchens made ready to move off, and our personal kits prepared for marching orders. Rumours on the cause of the wind-up ranged from increased emergency in Ireland to a German attack on the East Coast. The latter was regarded as the more likely. In fact nothing dramatic happened and on Monday the stand-by was called off.

On 1st August the home service status of the battalion was abolished and it was made available as a drafting unit, all trained hands being immediately assigned to the first overseas draft and detailed for draft leave the following week. The change was unexpected, but a radical revision of existing policy does not in retrospect appear surprising in view of current losses on the Somme, the magnitude of which had hardly yet struck home to us. Despite the earlier eager discussions when many had stated their fears of not getting to the front before the war ended, I noted that there were many among the chosen who failed to welcome the new situation.

We others were detailed at once for our first musketry course which commenced on 2nd August at the Birk Crag range. As this was the first time I'd fired anything more lethal than an airgun I felt somewhat apprehensive at the outset. But as soon as I had experienced the kick of the rifle, which our training had taught us effectively to counteract, all such apprehensions disappeared and I decided that shooting was good fun. The score in my Musketry Course Book at the end of the first day was quite good, but when the course was completed on 11th of the month my total fell a few points short of the minimum for First Class Shot and I never subsequently rose above the designation Second Class, due probably to an unnoticed defect in my long distance sight, something that the wall cards in the medical centres had failed to make clear. It was also no doubt disguised by my excellent sight at shorter ranges.

The butts at the picturesque Birk Crag range were sited ingeniously at varying levels across the valley, the firing position on one side, the targets on the other. As the ground was not private property much care had to be taken, by placing sentries, to keep civilian strollers and Strayers away from the danger zone when firing was in progress. When firing at 500 yards, with the targets high up the hillside, a number of cows wandered across on lower ground. One was seen to be shot, and later reports declared that two were hit. As the straying beasts were far below the line of fire, and although accident could not be ruled out, it was generally felt that the shooting was intentional. In fact a member of our group subsequently claimed to have been the perpetrator. He was a vindictive, unpopular type who was considered capable of anything underhand, but in view of his general incompetence in matters military we were doubtful about his capacity to do what he claimed, though there is still the possibility that his awkwardnesses were part of a calculated plan to prove his unsuitability for soldiering. It was he who left a round in his rifle, presumably after a burst of rapid fire, and nearly shot the inspecting officer who was carrying out the usual examination following such action. There was an official enquiry about the cows but no one was accused.

On the day we completed our course I was informed that I had been allocated to the second draft and would be given a pass for home leave the following day. As I had already become acclimatised to the vagaries of army life, the sudden change in outlook did not come as the surprise it might have done had I been able to look at the position from the outside. Clearly there had not been sufficient time to turn me and others of similarly short service into skilled fighting men. I knew that my peacetime companions had received much longer training than I had had, but at the same time I realized that the outlook in France had altered radically in the last few months. In any case there was nothing to be done about the matter.

That evening the first draft were given a gala dinner to which we were specially invited, an occasion that proved both entertaining and heartbreaking.

I went home on draft leave on 12th August. At that time only five days were allowed for that important, sad purpose. Apart from a visit to a theatre, I spent the time quietly. I walked across Wimbledon Common, so near to my home, and recognised that there, on our very doorstep was a stretch of countryside as beautiful as anything around Harrogate.

On the evening of the 16th we had a family reunion, which I was glad to get over, and on the following afternoon I left Kings Cross without having anyone to see me off, my definite choice, having always been harrowed when observing the heartrending farewells of others on such occasions. Parting is a very personal matter better done in private. That I returned to our northern camp with a heavy heart need hardly be stated, but how heavy were the hearts of youth on those occasions it would now be impossible to reinterpret in mere words. We reached the camp at 10.30 p.m. to find it deep in mud. The first draft had left the night before and had been due to reach France during the day.

The normal parades and exercises went ahead according to plan, interspersed with occasional visits to the company stores. On Sunday 20th there was another stand-to indicating, according to rumour, an immediate switch to the East Coast. Everything was packed for departure. Some advance groups from another brigade had left the night before. Within a few hours this stand-to also was cancelled. During the last week of our training we completed bombing instruction, which terminated with the throwing of two live Mills bombs from behind a specially constructed breastwork. Some of the men were so feckless that I pitied the instructors who had to stand by to cope with any emergency. The bombs provided a remarkably effective weapon, but I must say I always regarded them with apprehension even when the pin was firmly in position.

On the night of the 25th August our draft was entertained by the regiment. The menu included rabbit pie, peas and baked potatoes, plum pudding with cherry custard, beer and mineral waters, all in ample supply. It was served by the officers, who threw aside their class inhibitions and entered fully into the spirit of the occasion, approaching us in mock seriousness with such expressions as 'What would you like to drink, Sir?'. In print this may seem condescending, but in fact the keynote of the occasion was deep sincerity on all sides. Even the Sergeant-

Major had reassumed his humanity! We all knew too well what it was all about. The Colonel, who had himself lent a hand with the meal, gave an encouraging speech in which he told us that we were to join the Northumberland Fusiliers — 'The Fighting Fifth', a regiment with a military record second to none. But among ourselves we all agreed that we would have preferred to join our own first line battalion.

This celebratory occasion was followed the following evening by a special concert in the canteen, at which one of the more popular items was provided by Burko, the Conjuror. I noted that he was 'exceptionally clever', and from his publicity post-card which has survived, I see that the manipulation of playing cards was one of his specialities.

During the four days that remained our training continued, with senior staff officers taking a close interest in what we were doing. Even the Brigadier General attended the final bayonet assault course, assuring us that we had done very well. Our last Sunday was memorable. In the morning at the open air service the padre based his address on a theme which must have touched me as being very much to the point, for I noted it in my diary, a thing I had not done before, and was not to repeat later. It ran: 'The hypocrite of today is not the man that makes out he is better than he is, but he who makes out he is worse than he is.'

During the afternoon and evening, the glorious summer sun displaying the countryside at its best, I walked with Collet into the charming village of Ripley by way of Killinghall, returning via Hampsthwaite. Ripley, I noted, demonstrating an addiction to act the tourist inculcated by numerous seaside summer holidays, was a 'quaint cobble-stoned place' with a castle and old stocks. In its centre there was a stone monument (whose shape I outlined in pencil in the margin of my notebook) which was said to mark the spot where King Charles I killed a wild boar. Notably in the churchyard there was the Weeping Cross, which I queried as a well, said to be seventeen or eighteen centuries old.

On 29th August, the last day in our homeland, the parades continued at full pressure. Between 6.30 and 7.30 a.m. we were having our final bombing practices. The time from 9.00 to 11.30 was spent strenuously bayonet fighting on the final assault course, followed by thirty minutes of close order exercises. Between noon and 1.00 p.m. our kit was inspected by the Brigadier General, an unusually high level interest in such a procedure, who followed up with an address, no doubt to encourage us in our overseas enterprise, though I do not in fact recollect what it was all about. Our belongings had been increased by the addition of the identity disk which everyone on active service carried to facilitate identification should he become a casualty. It consisted of a round non-metallic disk with thin cord to encircle the neck. Mine was marked with my name, '7 N F R' and my number '7137'.

We were not allowed to slacken off after the midday meal. Between 2.00 and 3.30 p.m. the Divisional General was there to inspect us and watch us in a repeat performance over the bayonet assault course. Apparently he was satisfied. There was a pay parade at 4.00 p.m. at which I received seven shillings and my Active Service Pay Book which had to be carried on the person in future. There was also a special gift of cigarettes presented jointly by the CQMS and Private Richards, who had not been assigned to the draft. At 5.30 p.m. we delivered up our rifles, blankets and groundsheets, and received cap badge and shoulder titles of our new regiment, rifle oil, pipe, tobacco and writing pad. Captain Palmer then took us to the canteen for drinks and a further cigarette donation, and we were at last given a respite. Supper was served at 7.30 p.m. and the remainder of the evening was passed at a concert.

The draft fell in at 10.00 p.m. for roll call and to draw a day's rations. Now came the stage for saying goodbye, and there was not a dry eye among us all. This crowded and in every sense memorable twenty-four hours, so different in spirit from those that were to follow, when the anonymity of mass organization descended upon the earlier phase of the local unit, ended in a grand send-off through which we proceeded as in a dream. Handshakes and tears and heart-rending farewells; cheers along the route and from the crowds assembled outside the station at Harrogate. Though all too true it seemed unreal. In the glare of the station lamps, the regimental band playing our military march, the train drew out at 11.30 p.m. sharp into the darkness, towards the south and destiny.

HISTORICAL NOTE: GENERAL WAR SITUATION AND THE BATTLE OF THE SOMME UP TO SEPTEMBER, 1916

At the beginning of 1916, when the Great War had already been raging for seventeen months in all the continents — even America had had its battles of the Falklands — and across all the oceans of the world, a sort of military deadlock had been reached. To the original major contestants, Germany and Austria against Russia, France and the British Empire, other important nations had been added — Japan and Italy on the side of the Allies, Turkey on the side of Germany — and many smaller countries, in addition to the initially invaded victims of Belgium and Serbia, were gradually becoming involved. Despite the effective exploits of Germany's armed sea raiders, the world wide German colonial empire had been largely liquidated, while the Central Powers were being subjected, mainly by the Royal Navy, to a stringent and ever-tightening sea blockade, an action that was keeping a strongly neutralist United States well back from the sidelines.

One brilliantly conceived, badly co-ordinated and poorly commanded Allied attempt to deal decisively with Turkey and open a vital supplies route through the Dardanelles to isolated Russia, despite a heroic onslaught from the sea upon the Narrows by British, Anzac and French troops, had been frustrated by the stubborn resistance and inspired leadership of the defending Turks. Only the withdrawal in the night of the entire Allied force, almost without casualties, literally from under the noses of the victorious enemy, demonstrated what could be done by men who would not allow dire adversity to kill their spirit.

In the battles on the Western, Russian and Italian Fronts tremendous efforts had been made on both sides, battles lost and won and, particularly in Polish and Russian lands, vast wars of movement had been fought, all at a cost in hundreds of thousands of precious lives and mountains of sweat-produced guns, shells and other war supplies.

The general scene of deadlock was accentuated in the West — where the pundits were already declaring that the war was destined to be decided. Here there had been no substantial movement since the initial German drive had been halted, mainly by the French, at the Marne before the end of 1914.

By 1916 the cavalry was being kept well out of harm's way, while the infantry — already labelled the P(oor) B(loody) I(nfantry) — were being kept down like rabbits in their burrows by accurate machine gun fire, and kept apart by strong belts of almost impenetrable barbed wire, which the gradually mounting artillery barrages were finding even more difficult to clear than the concrete strong-points and shelters, in the construction of which the Germans were already showing themselves adept.

In December 1915 command of the British troops on the Western Front, where there was as yet no combined Allied command, had been taken over by Sir Douglas (later Earl) Haig, a position he was to hold, despite many vicissitudes at the front and intriguing cross-currents at home, for all the thirty-four months the war had still to run. He was almost immediately to be faced with planning an all-out offensive against the apparently impregnable enemy line. The British would have preferred this to take place on their northern flank which ran for a short way into Belgium, where success would have freed the Belgian coast, but this sector was totally unsuited to an offensive on the scale contemplated.

An area where the two Allied armies joined, across the valley of the River Somme, was chosen, and plans pressed ahead with a massive summer thrust in prospect. The Germans wisely decided by a counter stroke to pre-empt the expected Allied attack and to break the much weakened French resistance. They chose the strongly fortified Verdun Salient for their master blow and optimistically threw some of their best divisions into an all-out offensive to achieve a quick break-through. Despite their superior military skills, they had failed to draw the right conclusions from the outcome of the earlier slogging matches during 1915.

Verdun, a heroic memory to the French nation, was to become an anvil on which the German military power was to prove no match to human spirit and the elements, and both armies were to sacrifice the flower of a generation. At Verdun, each side was to suffer a total of three hundred thousand casualties. An immediate consequence was to render the Anglo-French campaign on the Somme necessary to relieve pressures at Verdun, to begin it earlier than had been planned, and to reduce the number of French divisions available to take part, as well as, of course, weakening the Germans' capacity to respond. As we already know, the date now fixed for the great offensive was 1st July, 1916.

In the meantime, despite the apparent stagnancy on the battle front, a stagnancy that hardly looked that way to the troops actively involved, events were not standing still, some with much greater consequence for the future than was apparent at the time. The German Zeppelin raids on England, which had already begun during 1915, were continuing with little more effect than to frighten the already frightened, murder and maim a number of innocents, and to reinforce the iron determination of the British people to resist. These raids also proved that as an instrument of war, the new-fangled air arm would have to depend upon the heavier than air plane rather than upon such a vulnerable target as the unwieldy dirigible, which one dauntless airman was to discover how to destroy with a well-directed burst from his machine gun.

Similarly in the homeland a rising by a small group of Irish Republicans centred in Dublin during the holy feast of Easter was ruthlessly suppressed and sixteen of the mainly youthful ringleaders were, after trial by courts martial, summarily shot. History was to prove this a tragic mistake, but at the time the idea that these youngsters should be given different treatment from that being meted out to men at the front for cowardice, desertion and treachery (according to the army code), would not have gone down very well with the troops there, including many thousands of Irish volunteers then taking part in the Empire's struggle. In fact the incident stirred little interest at a time when the Allied nations were literally struggling with their backs to the wall.

During the early spring peace initiatives were being taken by United States President Woodrow Wilson but the prospects were never bright. In May when at last it had become clear that the flow of volunteers was no longer likely to meet the insatiable demands of the battle front, Britain felt herself compelled to abandon the voluntary system and to introduce conscription, a move that was not very popular, even among troops who felt that every fit man should take a hand in the sad business from which the heroics of the early days had now departed.

In May also Admiral Jellicoe's Grand Fleet suffered considerable losses at the Battle of Jutland, and failed, largely through bad communications, to deliver the enemy a death blow, yet by driving the German Fleet back to its bases deprived it of offensive capacity until the end of the war, when it was to find its own watery grave in the cold waters of Scapa Flow. Of course the true position was not realised at the time and, despite retrospective disclosure of the hidden facts, controversy over the battle has raged ever since. In the vast complexities of the new type of world war the fruits of victory are not necessarily to be discerned in glowing exploits, for which, at the time, church bells may justly be tolled.

On 5th June Lord Kitchener, on a special mission to Russia which was greatly in need of aid from her Allies, was lost with the cruiser Hampshire when, stormbound off Scapa, it was sunk with all hands by a German mine. In his day he had been a great commander, and way back in the early months of the war his realistic assessment of the probable magnitude of the struggle and his appeals for patriotism, so brilliantly represented in a famous recruiting poster, had made a considerable impact on the imaginations of the young volunteers who literally stormed the recruiting stations throughout the land.

But as Minister of the Crown, among professional politicians adept at their jobs, his prestige had waned, although even in 1916 his death was taken almost as a personal affront by many of his grateful countrymen. At this time his great military contribution, the New Armies of Britain — Kitchener's Army — were being trained, and trained, and kept up to date with new techniques as they were reported back by old soldiers from the front, and the camps in Britain were teeming with healthy young men who were getting sick and tired of square bashing and bayonet fighting and the rest, and were still eager, despite all they had heard about the horrors of the trenches, to get at the enemy. Not that the services of the New Armies had been entirely neglected, for some of Kitchener's men had already proved themselves in France and Flanders and the Dardanelles, but now at last it was numbers that were to count. The curtain was about to rise on the greatest effort yet to break the formidable German line in France.

The strategically sited enemy trench line across the undulating meadowlands of the Somme river did not, to the distant observer, appear very formidable. But the deep well-planned trenches and sheltering dugouts, protected by heavy belts of barbed wire and reinforced at vital points with concrete emplacements and shelters — would have been a tough barrier to penetrate even without the devoted skills of the German machine-gunners, whose weapons were well placed to traverse across the open approaches of no man's land and to slice with scissors of fire the approaching infantry, many of them burdened with heavy equipment and gear.

The line chosen for the opening attack, stretched from Gommecourt on the British left to Soyecourt on the French right. The main thrust was to be shared by the British Fourth Army under General Rawlinson, with the support of some units of General Allenby's Third Army on his northern flank, and the French Sixth Army under General Fayolle on the right. At the outset the British forces comprised twenty-six divisions and the French thirteen: twelve and a half German divisions were said to have been involved on the opening day: many more were to be involved on both sides.

As was the custom at the time, the desultory but relentless Allied bombardment opened well in advance on 24th June, thus confirming what the enemy already sensed from his observations of the massive build-up going on behind the

Allied lines. While the heavies on the Allied side were not yet as powerful as they were to become later, as the howitzers came off the work lines at home, the barrage was considerable and rendered more potent by the mixing in of gas shells with the high explosives. The Allies had practical command of the air, then of primary importance only for observation, but from the very outset this was to be intermittently interrupted by the indifferent weather which was seriously to impede the course of the campaign.

On the appointed day, 1st July, 1916, the sun shone in a clear sky. Zero hour was at 7.30 a.m. Despite the havoc wrought by the preliminary bombardment, the German machine-gunners, rising literally from the ground like avenging devils, began to administer terrible punishment upon the confident British infantry as with enthusiastic discipline, they followed their officers over the parapet of the British trench line and advanced steadily in open order, as they had been trained to do. Particularly on the left flank, where little progress was to be made, the impact was shattering and the carnage heavy. The British right, however, made reasonable progress, reaching Fricourt, Mametz and Montauban after heavy fighting; while on the French front, where the Germans evidently had not expected a serious thrust, the operation was much more successful, a situation that was to continue for some time.

General Gough of the Fifth Army was immediately placed in command of the British left, to share the attack with General Rawlinson on his right. German resistance continued to be resolute and punishing, Fricourt was taken, and by the fifth day the line had reached La Boisselle and the outskirts of Contalmaison. The French thrust towards Combles continued to progress with but moderate losses.

By 7th July, with the enemy's first defence line in Allied hands, the desperate fighting continued into the well-devised fortifications of his second line, Contalmaison was captured, Mametz Wood cleared and most of Trones Wood taken. By this time British casualties alone had mounted to 90,000 and enemy losses could hardly have been much less.

Early on the morning of 14th July an all-out assault was launched on the German second line. The two Bazentins and the remainder of Trones Wood were taken, and during the following days the thrust continued painfully but relentlessly through Ovillers, Longueval, High Wood and Delville Wood, which the Germans defended literally foot by foot. At this juncture, when a threatening salient had been driven into the enemy line, the weather broke, movement became difficult and observation impossible. The Germans quickly took advantage of this lull and by 18th July were ready to counter-attack fiercely, gaining some of the lost ground and inflicting further heavy casualties. Five days later the British themselves counter-attacked, and after hard fighting Gough's troops on the left took strongly fortified Pozieres. By the end of the month Delville Wood had been completely cleared and Longueval captured, but Guillemont was still in German hands. Our total casualties had now risen to 160,000,

Already the great hopes for the offensive had been dashed. Never had armies before had to face such an ordeal and, apart from the evident sacrifice of the flower of a well trained voluntary army, the cost in ammunition and supplies already exceeded the most generous estimates: the factories were failing to turn out shells in the large quantities required to continue the battle. There was grave crisis on the home front. On the German side many more divisions had been drawn in and, as we were subsequently to learn, many of their units were in the depths of exhaustion, one of the objectives of the campaign, to relieve pressures elsewhere, having thus been achieved.

Bad weather and the need to regroup, to build up dumps, and to extend communications rendered further serious thrust impossible before the middle of August, when the attack on Guillemont and Thiepval was renewed. On 3rd September, Beaumont Hamel, Guillemont and Ginchy were attacked, while on the far right the French extended their flank southwards and pressed their advance on Peronne, one of the key-places in enemy hands.

At this juncture the German high commanders, Ludendorff and Hindenburg, who had replaced Falkenhayn, in conference on 8th September at Cambrai not far from the front, assessed the situation, realised that the exhaustion of their troops on the Western Front was reaching dangerous depths and, looking forward to the possible situation in 1917, decided to prepare a well-fortified line behind the existing front, employing all the ideas of military defence-construction which the Germans had rapidly acquired since the fighting had been driven inexorably into the ground and the defender had gained most of the advantage in this unprecedented type of warfare.

At the next major Allied attack on 15th September, between Le Sars and Morval, the primitive lozenge-shaped, tractored, motor vehicles, whose identity had been masked in manufacture under the label 'tank', took part for the first time, forty-seven of them in all. Their Wellsian appearance and weird antics surprised friend as much as foe. Good work was certainly done at Flers and Gueudecourt, where they lumbered across the German trench fortifications and cleared the enemy out as much by their terror-striking appearance as by their capacities as mobile machinegun fortresses.

This promising, but initially misused, British invention was to bring a new dimension into warfare, as the once irresistible, but now utterly vulnerable, cavalry had done in the distant past. But for the moment the very shell-torn nature of the ground it had been designed to traverse, was to prove too difficult and often too muddy for the tank to retain its mobility. Moreover our brave, cloistered, technically innocent tank-men still had everything to learn about the hazards of their dangerous new weapon, while the strategists who directed them had even more to learn about its tactical uses. The Germans evidently were not to be sufficiently impressed by its potentialities until it was too late for them to make use of tanks in that particular war, although the future was to show them as adept students of their inadvertent masters.

Another general attack on 25th September, supported by only thirteen of these fabricated monsters, penetrated the enemy line at the heavily fortified zone round Thiepval, that key-position, the ridge behind it and the two important village strongholds of Gueudecourt and Morval were taken, while the combined Allied forces captured the fortification of Combles and the immensely strong Stuff and Zollern Redoubts, in the assault upon and the defence of which heroic deeds were performed by the soldiers of both sides. But, as was to prove the case from now to the end of the Battle of the Somme, which still had two months to go, the weather was to intervene more and more effectively.

It was at this stage, when hope of a breakthrough had become very thin and the fighting — if that is the proper word for it in a battle situation when neither friend nor foe saw anything of one another except as prisoners — was to run hopelessly into the mud, that the present writer, a young inadequately trained infantryman became an active member of a sadly disenchanted cast. The present book recounts his experiences during that depressing final stage of the great Battle of the Somme which numerous general accounts have often failed adequately to cover. One could hardly do better in concluding this historical note, than to quote Lieut-Colonel John Baynes's recent summing up [in History of the First World War, Vol. 4, No. 13, p. 1686 (Purnell 1969-71)]:

> To the men who fought through these two autumn months it was remembered as one of the most exhausting and dismal periods of the whole of the First World War. The mud of the Somme during the wet weather of October 1916 was never to be forgotten by those who struggled and suffered through it.

II: THE BASE

Some comparatively unimportant happenings remain engraved in memory. Although so many eventful years have passed since the 30th August 1916, I remember the opening impressions of that day more clearly even than the happenings of last week. It began in a railway carriage. I was jolted into consciousness as the train ran on to a bridge: through half-opened lids I discerned in dim silhouette the dome of St. Paul's. The indefinite picture rapidly composed itself in my mind and I realized with sinking heart that this was my last fleeting glimpse, perhaps for ever, of the city in which I had lived since my parents had emigrated from Reading in my infancy. Away to the west the Thames flowed past Putney, my home and all I held dear. In that crowded train I felt wretchedly alone and painfully homesick. My mind groped its way back over my nineteen sheltered years.

My reverie ended. The train rattled on through London's sprawling suburbs and away to the south. From the racks above our equipments overflowed and the entrenching tool handles jangled with every lurch. My khaki-clad companions gradually stirred from their grotesque sleeping postures. By my side Jimmy Downs, my established pal, his face with its small indefinite moustache, pale and serious, twitched nervously awake. On the opposite seat young Martin, reputed to have intentionally shot the cow which inadvertently strayed across the range at Birk Crag, continued to sleep, his tired sallow face looking even less healthy than usual. Soon the compartment was all a-bustle. The time for dreams had passed.

Our destination, though we did not know it until we arrived, was Shorncliffe. After a welcome breakfast of tea, bacon, bread dipped in the fat, at the rest camp up on the cliffs, we were marched to Folkestone along the coast road past gaily beflagged villas and knots of cheering townsfolk who, surprisingly, even at this stage of the war, did not take for granted this frequently recurring sight. Upon us, with spirits needing little excuse to sag, this heartening reception had an encouraging effect: we even went aboard our transport — the S.S. *Victoria*, one of the old cross-channel steamers — with an air of cheerfulness that was not entirely counterfeit. But we were leaving our hearts behind.

The weather was dull and squally. Our veneer of cheerfulness soon peeled away. For my part, uplifted by a feeling of superiority through having once visited Boulogne by excursion in the *Brighton Queen*, the swell of the waters was matching my mood. I came very near enjoying the crossing. Our draft was soon in poor shape: packed like sardines, symptoms of sickness quickly appeared and the general discomfort increased. Most of my companions were too preoccupied to notice the grim shape of our destroyer escort as it drove in the middle distance over the swelling waves. Few of us in those days had journeyed so far from home.

At Boulogne we disembarked in a steady downpour, to be straightway drawn up in double rank along the quay in front of the Post Office, and then to be manoeuvred about in the usual leisurely, exasperating way, while rain soaked into our packs and equipments and ran off the edges of our groundsheets. We cursed the rain, we cursed the men who could not forgo a single manoeuvre that was laid down in King's Regulations, and we cursed the fate that had brought us to this depressing place. Thus our great adventure began.

The rain had stopped by the time we started the climb out of the town to the Rest Camp on the cliffs where we were to spend our first nights in France. Those first impressions were most unfortunate, though I cannot say that they were greatly out of tune with so much that we were to experience during the next few months. Just out of the town we passed a row of wretched cottages and I remember still my surprise at seeing and smelling the filthy garbage in the gutter in front of them. Was this *la belle France* about which we had heard so much?...

A couple of miles or so from Boulogne the four immense lattice steel wireless masts that dominated the Rest Camp came into sight, towering high above a confusion of stunted huts and tents and large marquees. We were assigned for the night to a roomy hut, bare of any furniture, and a small batch of us moved off with the grudging step of the impressed fatigue party to draw blankets and rations from the store. The blankets were issued at once but the rations, we were annoyed to discover, were for issue the next day. Our reception had certainly not been organized to create a good impression, and our new abode had little to commend it.

I had no difficulty in persuading Jimmy that this was the occasion for a scrounge. We were both very hungry and we had already grasped the added disadvantage of staying in the hut, where some sort of fatigue might be sprung upon loiterers at any moment. Our instinct led us in the direction of a large hut boldly marked with the letters E.F.C. which we quickly discovered stood for Expeditionary Force Canteen. Stacked on shelves and overflowing on to the counter that ran along one side of the canteen was a magnificent display of foodstuffs — canned fruit and meats, cake, biscuits, chocolate, sandwiches — as well as cigarettes, beer, tea and other drinks. We soon forgot our tiredness and lost our hunger.

When we paid for our purchases we were intrigued to learn that in crossing to France, sixpence in silver had become seven pennies in copper, whether English or French. This freak of the exchange was to cause a good deal of brain-racking among the customers and I suspect that the lucky E.F.C. men, who always looked well-groomed and fed, occasionally made a small profit out of the confusion. This was my first practical instruction in economics, a subject whose very title was then beyond my ken.

After roll-call at 8.30 p.m. we did our best to make a comfortable bed for two on the bare floor, and would have been comparatively successful had not the rain recommenced and poured through every weak spot in the roof. Our first dawn in France was miserable enough. Reveille was at 5.30 a.m. and there was plenty of time to wash and smarten ourselves up. We were quite ignorant of the day's programme. For the moment the centre of attraction was a group of men of the Royal Marine Artillery down from the line who regaled us with far from reassuring tales of the trenches, until the arrival of our scanty breakfast. The battle-marked warriors, speaking of their experiences under fire, belonged to a different breed whom I approached with awe. My fearfulness of the future was tempered by a genuine naivety about the front that would hardly seem credible to a later hard-bitten generation.

At 9.30 a.m. there was the routine medical inspection, an experience to which we had been too frequently subjected in camp at home to cause any surprise. We stood with chests bared and arms outstretched before us, while the medical officer, his face fixed in a supercilious stare, passed down the ranks as fast as he could walk. If he had wanted to create an impression of inhumanity he could hardly have done it more effectively. However, all this was in the accepted pattern of those days: human relations were hardly understood in an army brought up to consider toughness the supreme virtue. If we civilian soldiers in the main had sufficient guts to conform outwardly to the established pattern, our hearts were too soft not to feel poignantly the callousness of the machine and to sink to the very depths of despair even before any real ordeal had befallen us.

The day was bright. The view from the camp over the sea was magnificent. During the morning we were assigned to bell-tents and felt more at home. I was able to write my first letter to Blighty, as we were now privileged to call the beloved country we had left behind. There was no question of wandering over the countryside for we were confined to camp. During the afternoon, however, men of many drafts, amounting to some thousands, were marched with bands playing into the town, a propaganda parade to impress our allies with the flow of reserves still pouring across the Channel. They had recently had plenty of disappointing news from the front to dampen their spirits.

Of all the army routines I always found the route march the least irksome. Within the pattern of the marching column, in four files as was then the custom, there was a good deal of freedom — to think, at least — to talk and sing and to enjoy the changing scene. That afternoon, as we marched along the heights in the sunshine, the white cliffs of Dover clearly fringed the distant horizon. It was a melancholy sight and the momentary air of depression at what might well be the last sight of our native land, was poignantly expressed by the silence that fell upon the khaki files as we swung down into Boulogne.

Yet by the time we reached the Porte de Calais all melancholy was forgotten: we were merrily, if not always tunefully, singing the latest favourites: 'Pack Up Your Troubles' and 'Take Me Back to Dear Old Blighty'. The sidewalks were thronged and a number of the men were soon practising their first halting phrases in French, much to the amusement of the townsfolk. Others shouted coarse invitations in English, which it is to be hoped were not fully understood. Needless to say, we all returned from this brief excursion in much better mood than when we set out.

Our second morning in the camp was spent in idling round the bell-tents. Characteristically some of the boys improvised a band with mouth-organs and empty biscuit tins while we all joined in chorus. 'Way Down in Tennessee' and 'A Long, Long Trail...' were sung with feeling but neither could compete with 'I Want to go Home'. I had first heard this lugubrious ditty at Harrogate, sung by blue-clad wounded soldiers from the convalescent hospital. I do not remember the precise words but they ran something like this:

> I want to go home, I want to go home
> I don't want to go to the trenches no more
> Where 'minniewerfer'[1] screech and cannon do roar
> Take me over the sea, where the Alleman cannot catch me
> Oh my, I don't want to die, I want to go home.

I listened to the refrain in that peaceful English setting with a sense of shame and distaste, tempered by a naive wonder that those whom I regarded as heroic could voice such sentiments. Yet I do not recollect that a mere month or two later I joined in with any less gusto than did the others. The song clearly conveyed a truth deep in our souls that we could not have put into more orthodox terms. We were already, even before the experience of truth had fallen upon us, members of a different

---

[1] *Minenwerfer* (Ger).

world. We were already divided from those we loved by the psychological barrier that existed during the Great War between the men at the front and their civilian brothers.

When our throats had become sore and our enthusiasm for music had somewhat flagged we, Jimmy and I, agreed to complete a four of whist, while many of our companions, sprawling around in the sunshine, grappled with a little handbook *How to Speak French* which they had bought in the canteen. Sad to relate, these early linguistic efforts were in most cases destined to be a mere flash in the pan. The phrases *bon jour* and *parlez vous* were in the main the limits beyond which these experiments were rarely carried. The stagnant nature of the battle-front made it quite unnecessary for the authorities to encourage any further efforts in this direction.

At 2.00 p.m. the several drafts paraded and entrained at the railway siding for an unknown destination. Packed in cushionless third class compartments of a French train it was an hour before we departed and the journey of some fifteen miles occupied another two and a half hours. It was the inconsequential aimlessness of such army movements that annoyed me almost beyond endurance, coupled with the fact that we were never — at that period, at any rate — told what we were doing. Fortunately it was a lovely sunny afternoon and as the train puffed along hesitatingly it was possible to jump off and even to gather some of the flowers that covered the embankments. This we found extremely amusing, but we had plenty to damp our spirits at the end of our journey. Our destination was Etaples where among the sand dunes an immense base had been set up. Few of us had heard of the place before, either in war or peace when it had been just a quiet and attractive little seaside resort.

At the encampment we were immediately sorted into detachments, for we came from many regiments and were going to many different battalions. Members of the first Hertfordshire draft were there to meet us and many hearty greetings were exchanged between old friends. They had left Harrogate some weeks before and were still awaiting drafting to the line. We discovered, however, that we had been brought to Etaples for training and we were promised a pretty rough time in the process.

There was also a different sort of reception committee whose impact I was never to forget. A motley khaki crowd of nondescript troops collected near the station exit, upon our approach raised a bantering cry of 'More for the slaughter-house', accompanying it with gibes and sneers at the lateness of our arrival. Just who they were I never knew — probably wounded men from the line, convalescing at the base camp and disgruntled at not getting home — but theirs was a most depressing welcome calculated to reduce our already drooping spirits to zero. I do not remember anything like it happening at any other time and have no doubt there was some special explanation for the occurrence. The old hands were habitually too sorry for the inexperienced to add insult to injury in this way, but the terrible Somme battle had been in progress since 1st July and failure to exploit the situation had caused a cloud of disappointment to settle over the Western Front.

As we left the station we were marched straightaway through an adjacent arms store, where we received new vaseline-daubed short Lee-Enfield rifles in place of the long training pattern which we had relinquished before leaving Harrogate. Our immediate destination proved to be that sector of the camp assigned to Northumberland Fusilier reinforcements, known officially as the 32nd Infantry Base Depot.

Here the Camp Adjutant, in his red-banded hat, was waiting impatiently to inspect and then to harangue us inhumanly on the punishments that would inevitably follow any dereliction of duty. He informed us, almost with fervour, that if we slept on sentry we should most certainly be shot and then went on to explain the dire penalties involved in the award of No. 1 Field Punishment. Any remaining spirit thus having been completely eliminated, we were set to pitch our own bell-tents on a strip of ground between the permanent huts of the depot and the parade ground. Two blankets per man were issued from a dump at the end of the lines and we were left to fend for ourselves. It was now well past the normal mealtime and there was no question of special provisions for the newcomers. Our natural reaction was to smarten ourselves up and go in search of a canteen.

On the following morning we were awakened at 5.30 a.m. by the sound of many bugles; within a quarter of an hour, half-awake in the grey light of the tent, we were called out and drawn up for roll call. That first day at the base was typical of the army, with much bustle and many alarms and altogether not a lot done. We were first ordered to prepare for inspection, and there followed much cleaning of rifles and equipment. The removal of surplus vaseline from the former was no easy task with the means at our disposal. We paraded in full marching order, were marched back and forth, inspected and re-inspected until at last the General Officer Commanding made his appearance. The traditional ceremony was then carried through.

During the performance one man collapsed in the ranks and had to be carried away. I thought this a terrible thing to happen, an affront to all the military codes, one of those things that we had been taught to regard as beyond the pale. I prayed that it would never happen to me. But as the victim disappeared from sight and the great man began to walk along the ranks other thoughts forced themselves into my mind. Obviously the stricken soldier was ill. How ill? Possibly too ill to go further towards the line. If that were the case, not pity but envy would be my natural reaction. I could envy any man, however dire his lot, who, as by the wave of a magic wand, got his release from army life, which my few months in uniform had taught me was little different from prison. After this silly useless parade, when all the things had been done according to the regulations, we were again subjected to medical inspection, which was just as formal and even less satisfactory than any before.

During the afternoon we were taken for a short march of five or six miles through a countryside that was drab and uninteresting, and only more attractive than the camp in having about it a sense of freedom. We were not allowed to visit Etaples on our own. This was not a busy day after the urgent early start. No doubt we were being settled in. First impressions were being confirmed. The camp was a regular town of huts with a sprinkling of marquees and bell-tents. It impressed me as something of a replica, not intentional of course, of one of those Wild West lumber camps that I had so often seen in the cinema or read about in tales of Buffalo Bill, so popular among the youth at that time. A waste of dunes had been converted into a bustling hive of men in drab khaki. Streets criss-crossed in all directions and traffic — horse-drawn waggons, gun limbers, etc. — was regulated by military police stationed at the more important crossings.

Our meals were served in a large dining hut near the depot. The food itself was good enough but the method of serving it was shocking even by army standards. Each man entered, armed with knife, spoon and fork, and selected a vacant seat at one of the long unwashed benches. If none was vacant one had to await the next round; consequently there was always a mad dash for the first sitting. The orderlies — base wallahs, as we came to know them — of long experience, rushed round ladling the food from large churns into plates and bowls which could have done with a good scrub. The tables were usually covered with filth from previous sittings, and the atmosphere stank of stale food and crowded humanity. It was not a place to dally in.

On the brighter side this seething morass of humanity had its numerous rest huts run by the Church Army, the Young Men's Christian Association and other organizations, as well as the ubiquitous Expeditionary Force Canteens. These were equipped for rest periods with games rooms and quiet rooms, the latter being well supplied with newspapers and magazines. There one could write home, buy a cup of tea, and perhaps chat with one of the padres or social workers who devoted their time to bringing a note of friendliness into the arid military atmosphere of the place.

For the more thoughtful there were even lectures. While I was at the Base I listened to talks on 'Nationality and Empire' and 'Bismarck', not the sort of topics that the troops themselves would have chosen, but well enough delivered and illustrated to attract good and attentive audiences, many of whose members were no doubt nostalgically transported to a fairer world from which we seemed already to be parted by some impassable gulf. The more imaginative of us knew that we had crossed into a sort of Purgatory which would shortly change into Inferno. In this camp there were many who had been beyond and returned. To me at least they inspired a feeling of wonder, without creating any urge to emulation.

On the following day our training began in earnest. We discovered the 'Bull Ring'. Known officially as No. 2 Training Camp, this minor hell, sited among the sand dunes bordering the sea, comprised a series of training grounds, more or less naturally separated by space and the higher dunes, amidst which the most up-to-date training impedimenta had been set up. There were an immense levelled parade ground, numerous drill enclosures, bayonet courses, and practice grounds for bomb throwing, rifle marksmanship, Lewis gun practice and the rest. The situation was pleasant enough and from the parade grounds by the seashore the scene over the estuary across the sandy ridge had a beauty all its own. Peacefully in the distance the little resort of Paris Plage, nestling along the shore, brought into our artificial military world a feeling of otherness that made at least one of the practising band sick with thoughts of home. Prisons should be surrounded by sights that match their own sour purposes.

There were two ingredients that made the place worse than need be — the sand and the 'canaries'. The sand was everywhere, rendering the simplest military evolution, to which we had already become inured at home, an act of great labour. The 'canaries', thus irreverently named because of the bright yellow armlet which was the mark of their special authority, were the commissioned and non-commissioned officers to whom the tasks of training had been committed. Most of them had come from the front, a fact that they treated without modesty. Their manner, with a few exceptions, was immoderate and irascible; their aim no doubt to break us in in the shortest possible time. Efficiency one could respect, and I never personally objected to the discipline of the parade ground, especially when it was really successful in producing that machine-like response which the new recruit in particular is so proud to achieve.

But there was here a pervading touch of officiousness, as though these minions had some private fear which they were trying hard to master. This manifestation swelled to a veritable crescendo on the very first morning as we completed our tasks and the whole parade marched past the General Officer Commanding who had taken up a review position at the entrance to the camp. Along our flanks, as we marched with our rifles at the slope, the canaries ran like a pack of snapping dogs, shouting and bawling at us as though to draw from their master the only favour that they treasured in all the world. The prize of immunity was certainly great but the price in sycophancy heavier than I could have paid.

Taking it all round, our training, which continued almost daily until 11th September, seemed effective. Its main object was to provide us with the latest experience from the battle-front; there was much that had been impressed upon us in England as constituting the finality of military truth, which we now had to unlearn. An attempt was made in some of the courses to reproduce the conditions of the battlefield, the germ no doubt of battle training that was to be the normal feature of the later war. We practised bayonet fighting on arduous courses with a variety of suspended and grounded sacks; we practised bomb throwing; we were lectured on health and water arrangements.

One day after a truly frightening lecture on the horrors of gas warfare, during which we were told how the poor devils up in the Ypres Salient had first met this new terror in 1915, some by soaking primitive self-made respirators in urine, the class was subjected to the real thing. Each man wearing his cloth respirator had to grope through a covered trench filled with a concentration of poison gas which we were told was many times stronger than anything we could possibly meet in the open. The experience certainly served to give us confidence. One of the draft, it is true, fainted in the gas chamber and had to be hauled to safety, but this was from nerves and not gas.

I felt even at the time that too much was being made of this horror, and my subsequent experiences never led me to believe that poison gas was in the same category as high explosive either in practical effect or sheer frightfulness. None of us was much taken with the respirator of that period — p.h. helmet, I think it was called — which was a sticky, chemically treated cloth bag, with goggles and mouthpiece, that covered one's head and was made air-tight by buttoning down under the tunic. These helmets were not easy to adjust and were never popular, but they certainly stood up to the test until something better was forthcoming. We carried them in a little green cloth satchel slung separately over our equipment.

One evening we participated in night operations in a trench system realistically constructed to represent an actual battlefield. There a miniature battle was enacted with attack and counterattack. Smoke bombs were thrown and blank cartridges fired, and our reactions were observed. Even the least military-minded of us enjoyed this descent into play-acting and in the dusk, with few senior eyes upon them, our canary-tutors became almost human.

All the time at the Bull Ring things were happening. One day we were being drilled near the live-bombing range. Pieces of bomb casing frequently buzzed and spluttered over the dunes, occasionally ricocheting into the sand over which we were being manoeuvred.

The instructor, continuing without apparent concern, ridiculed us for being jumpy, particularly when drawn up at attention. 'Stand still, you bleeders. The shrapnel's spent and carn't 'urt a fly. You'll know all erbout it when you get among the real stuff.'

He had hardly stopped bawling when a piece of flying metal hit one of the draft, lacerating two fingers so seriously that he had to be taken to the dressing tent — our first casualty. But such incidents were common. Attached to the Base there was already a considerable cemetery. Recently a soldier in another draft had had his thumb knocked off by the cocking handle of a Lewis gun: his own carelessness indeed, but the penalty was death from lockjaw. During one of the bayonet practices a member of our own draft, jumping down into a trench to stab the sack at the bottom, accidentally slipped and ran on to his own bayonet. He was carried to the hospital in a serious condition. We were thus learning the cheapness of life, just a little ahead of the reality.

Despite the pervading drabness of brown sand and khaki uniforms the camp was not without its lighter side. It happened that the weather during those early September days was fine and one could not be long in the camp at off-parade times without becoming aware of shouting groups of men, squatting on the sand round some centre of interest. A game of House was in progress. This was the only officially approved game in which money was allowed to change hands. It was in fact the children's game of Lotto whose sets of green squared cards and numbered counters were sold neatly boxed in the toy shops at home. (Since then it has been resurrected on a wide scale as Bingo.) The undoubted popularity of this innocuous pastime at that time and place was a clear indication that its devotees had nothing better to do. The shouting came mainly from the organizers, who were allowed a percentage of the takings for their pains, the bulk however being re-distributed to the holder of the winning card.

'Housey, Housey, Who'll have a buckshee card?' shouts one of the organizers, his voice raised to counter similar cries from neighbouring groups. A free round is offered at the outset to all who will take a card. The prize on this occasion is five francs, paid out of previous takings. Each school has at least two organizers, one to issue and check the cards, the other to draw the numbered pieces from the little bag in which they have been shaken. Each card has a different series of numbers printed between the little green squares. The players sit round on the sand intently watching their cards and marking them with pieces of chalk or broken matches whenever one of their numbers is drawn from the bag, as announced by the drawer. The player whose card is first completed shouts 'house' and wins the game.

It was a simple game calling for a minimum of intelligence in the player, whose participation was purely passive, although it was of course possible for the slow-witted to miss a number and thus fail to claim the prize. Some touches of the picturesque were added by the organizers who often disclosed a flair for humorous repartee. They had evolved a special intonation for calling the numbers, like priests of a new cult, and some of the numbers were given special names, partly no doubt to prevent confusion. Thus the sequence of called numbers might have run 'Twenty-three'; 'Number Ten'; 'Doctor's Pill' (9); 'Clickety-click' (66); 'Blind Forty' (40); 'Top O'th'Box' (90); 'Fifty-seven'; 'Kelly's Eye' (1), and so forth, the first word always being strongly accented.

As likely as not, just round the corner in the lea of a marquee or hut, there was another and much quieter game in progress. Someone, breaking all the rules, had put down a Crown and

Anchor board and much larger sums were involved. I had not been long in the camp before I saw it all happen. The gamester, on this occasion a member of the Army Service Corps whose generous scale of pay no doubt facilitated the financing of this under-the-cover activity, came to his pitch looking furtively in all directions before unrolling his sheet of green baize with its six divisions marked with an ace, an anchor or a crown — the devices on the six sides of the dice. All the time, while encouraging his clients to make their bets, the showman kept up a continuous but highly stereotyped patter: 'Come along, me lucky lads, bang it down thick and heavy.' 'If you don't speculate you can't accumulate.' 'Have a little bit on the old sergeant-major.' The odds naturally were on the bank but luck could run against the banker. Gambling left me cold and I could therefore look on dispassionately while others recklessly drained out their few hardly earned francs. On this occasion one of the canteen-men came along, no doubt well enough off not to need to bother about losing a few francs. He put down heavy stakes and having an unusual run of fortune soon broke the bank, much to the delight of the bystanders who were not used to seeing funds flow in this direction.

But for these pastimes, permitted and forbidden, and the numerous recreation huts, there was little in the camp to cheer the troops. The only women to be seen wore nurses' uniform, except for a small number of French stall-holders, countrywomen from the village, who were allowed to set up booths just inside the main entrance to sell souvenirs. Those that attracted us most, and for which indeed there was always a ready sale, were the fancy postcards with a decorative silk panel displaying pretty designs and greetings similar to anniversary cards at home. They were a boon to the inarticulate. It would be interesting to know how many hundred thousand of these pretty trifles were sent to Britain during the war, and how many still survive, possibly in some closely guarded drawer, evidence of a heartbreak that a life's memory has been unable to efface.

Although letter-writing and reading were for most of us our dearest and most constant recreation, we were, I imagine, generally an inarticulate army. It was a recurring experience, in the day sitting at the entrance of a tent or at night crouching by the dim light of a candle, to see the all-absorbed khaki figure writing with varying fluency to a beloved one across the sea, and in the evenings many of us found in one of the rest huts a quiet corner for the same purpose. Other attractions, so far as they existed, were of secondary importance except for the orphaned and the illiterate.

Our correspondence was carried home without postal charge. Yet, quite apart from the natural self-consciousness of youth, I could never divest myself of the knowledge that my letter would be read by a censor before it reached its recipient. In addition, there was the absolute need to leave out all references to place or military action, and there was the ever-present feeling that one's personal life was being pried into. All letters were then censored by an officer of ones own unit, but later I was to discover the Green Envelope, which put the writer on his honour not to convey information of military importance and was only subjected to test censorship at a distance, by individuals with whom one was not acquainted.

There was also the Field Post Card with a set of laconic remarks about one's health and welfare which could be deleted as appropriate. These were quickly filled in and could be despatched without delay whenever time was short and inspiration lacking. If they reduced the process of communication on the sender's side to an impersonal routine, the mere arrival of one of these cards no doubt often brought a feeling of reassurance to the recipient that was out of all proportion to the effort of the sender. What more did those at home want to know than that the absent one was still in the land of the living? — a fact that the stereotyped card indicated as clearly as the longest missive.

Fortunately there was normally no censorship of mail or papers in the opposite direction and no more welcome official existed than the post corporal who appeared usually at some routine time to call out the names of those for whom he had some mail. It was indeed a moment of great delight when I received my first few lines from home and a packet of newspapers some days old. This event took place on 8th September, the tenth day after our departure overseas.

Yet the very receipt of letters and news from home served to accentuate the gap between our two worlds. We lived now in an atmosphere of rumour which we both believed and doubted. A few days earlier the camp had been heartened by a report that a Zeppelin had been brought down over England. Nothing was more deprecated in those days than the enemy's war on the civilian population, a policy on his part that had been manifest from the very first hours when Belgium was invaded. Nothing therefore gave us more heart than the news that such attempts had been bloodily frustrated. We regarded these attacks as against all the civilization that we knew — and so they were in the world as it had been.

At the base camp we were of course continually aware of the great battle still in progress beyond the northern horizon whence sometimes we felt we could hear the distant rumble of the guns. The papers from home added detail to this threatening background of our potentially transient lives. But while we thought in terms of insecurity and death, the war correspondents were still adept at finding victory in every few yards of enemy-occupied territory retaken, and the practice of ignoring movements the other way created an overall impression that a cumulative gain was constantly progressing in the direction of Berlin.

In truth the battle-front was at the moment marking time. Of the spirit of the troops reports were always glowing — of course we liked to be praised — but in the light of our own reactions and the somewhat clouded countenances of those around us we soon became very cynical over the constantly reiterated assertion that the British troops were filled with eagerness to get at the Hun. Not that this was a sudden discovery on my part. Had I not ever in my mind the dirge of the Harrogate wounded? Had I not from the very first days of the war been an omnivorous reader of the many reports from the front by which we had been flooded. Newsprint was not in short supply. Histories of the war had commenced publication immediately, in weekly and fortnightly parts, and numerous special magazines were devoted to the war in all its aspects.

If the sketches of the war artists were usually too sensational to convey the real situation at the front, photography soon came to the aid of the pencil to enable even the least imaginative to realise something of the truth. Only the noise and the smell were missing. Although I was still extremely naive in my interpretation of the experience in which I was about to be involved, I had few illusions about the depths of horror that lay behind those journalistic portrayals.

The overriding need for secrecy in the face of possible espionage was no doubt the main reason why we were given so little information about our future movements, and were prevented from disclosing to those at home the little we did know. We were not allowed to possess cameras and photography was forbidden to all except accredited press photographers, whom we would rarely, if ever, see. In any case it is doubtful whether members of the ranks could have afforded folding cameras, though it may be that an officer could have smuggled one in his kit, with the connivance of the orderly who was assigned to look after him. Diaries too were not permitted to be carried, which is understandable in terms of their value to the enemy if one were captured. Yet this rule I disobeyed, my one conscious default from Army Regulations. But I conformed to the spirit of the law by confining my brief entries to the personal and avoiding the least geographical reference. I felt that it would not be difficult to expand my notes afterwards should I survive. I recollect that I made little effort to conceal what I was doing and no doubt I was unconsciously wise in this for an attitude of secrecy draws attention to itself. I may have been assisted by the fact that my erstwhile colleagues were not themselves addicted to the habit.

If other diaries were kept in my immediate circle I was not aware of it, and in view of the fact that the personal belongings of fatalities were carefully collected and sent to the next of kin it is unlikely that had such a practice been widespread it would have escaped notice. I kept my small stiff-covered note-book in the left-hand breastpocket of my tunic over my heart, a flimsy yet reassuring shield.

Although the whole atmosphere of the camp was tensed for the predominant purpose of preparing us for battle and we woke every morning with the query 'Is this the day?', the hour of departure was kept secret. Yet on the day our first post arrived there were other incidents that might well have indicated a change in the flow of events.

The first, which took place during the night, certainly had no connection with our future unless it were an augury we were not competent to read. This was the collapse of a large canteen which had just flattened out, fortunately without hurting anyone. Such an untoward incident, pointless as it may have been, was the topic of the most eager conversation and many were the theories offered to explain how and why it had happened. It was, I think, the sheer casualness of the incident that confounded us, for we had begun to feel that nothing could happen in this depressing place that was not related to the business in hand. The crash at least suggested that unplanned things could occur and the great interest in the matter of so small importance indicated a sense of relief that few of us could have put into words at the time.

There was, however, another happening that had a much closer bearing upon our fate. Our first draft left suddenly to join the Royal Sussex in the line. They had preceded us to France by some weeks, a much more carefully selected group, and their protracted stay at Etaples filled us with a certain hope that our own departure could not be imminent. Now they were no longer there to act as a sort of bulkhead between us and the inevitable.

Two days later a further step in our matriculation for battle took place. Following a medical inspection, which was rather more seriously undertaken than the preceding ones, a few of the draft were marked to stay at the base; a fate that most of us secretly envied.

Young Chapman, at least, among the chosen had no such feelings. Some personalities, like some events, impress themselves upon our minds when others have vanished like dreams. Chapman was of the former type. Although I had little to do with him personally I remember him as a cheerful, dynamic and essentially honest youth. Apart from an enduring impression of his appearance and personality, the only detail that lingers is an anecdote which he retailed on one of the numerous occasions when conversation turned to the perennial topic of the opposite sex. Chapman told how, when returning one night from leave in an ordinary railway carriage, a well-dressed girl on the opposite seat, a stranger to him, pulled up her skirts shamelessly but invitingly to display her person. To those who were as innocent as Chapman, the incident was an affront to an idealist view of womanhood which then could have a fairy-tale quality likely to be considered absurd today. No doubt with many of us the shock was largely eclipsed by a genuine disappointment that no such experience had come our way. That I should remember so clearly such a trivial matter amidst a jumble of much less savoury memories is due, I think, to the fact that Chapman was the teller. Only such as he could have conveyed to those of his own type such an incident without lascivious imputations or the suspicion of romancing. His brief encounter had implications we could sense without fully understanding.

Chapman was certainly not pleased at authority's latest decision. A bantam in appearance and full of pluck he was one of the few who were genuinely eager to join the battle. He was also among those who had falsified their age to the recruiting sergeant. Now, at this late stage, his parents, exercising their legal right, managed to impose a veto on his going to the front before his nineteenth birthday. The prospect of cooling his heels amidst the dreary sands of Etaples gave him no pleasure. Nevertheless, his parents were right and, even if their action had saved him but a few months of the horror of the trenches, it was to good purpose. Whether it achieved more than that amount of grace I do not know, for I never met Chapman again.

The following day brought the luxury of a shower-bath in a specially equipped hut. I had thoroughly hated the first occasion for communal bathing of this sort in England, but modesty is the first casualty of army life and the sheer pleasure of standing in warm running water overwhelmed my normal diffidence amidst so much nudity and the slightly nauseous odour of massed humanity. The future was closing in upon us, for, apart from the welcome cleansing water, we were this day also bathed in an ominous tide of rumour. Movement was in the air.

That same evening, as I returned from the large YMCA hut alongside the railway where I had enjoyed an interesting lecture on 'England in the Time of Shakespeare', I noticed among the tents a figure that seemed familiar. But his profile was turned away as he leant over the letter he was writing and I was not sure. Hesitatingly I came back again and in the head now raised from his task I recognized Clough, a colleague from my office, a fellow assistant clerk from the Contracts Section of the Post Office Stores Department in Bedford Street, just off the Strand.

He was a quiet somewhat reserved type, looking very different in his khaki, his face somewhat white and drawn. We welcomed each other eagerly and wondered why we had not met before. He had belonged to our Hertfordshire's sister battalion, which, after a spell at Soham had joined us on the moors of Harrogate. Tomorrow his draft was leaving to join the Duke of Wellington's in the line. He was sick at heart at the prospect, disliking army life as much as I did. We arranged to exchange letters — but did so only briefly for soon I failed to receive a reply. It was some months later that I learned he had been killed within a few weeks of joining his regiment, a not unusual fate those days.

On my arrival back at the tent, which we shared with eight others, Jimmy told me there was a strong rumour that we were to join a labour battalion. We were not very clear about the meaning of this, for the existence of special labour battalions was news to us. There was certainly a general impression that it was not very creditable to have this sort of allocation, as the decision seemed to place a stigma on our quality as fighting troops. However, after a good deal of talk right up to 'lights out' the consensus was that if it meant a somewhat better chance of survival we could bear the implied ignominy philosophically.

Rumour for once proved correct. Early the next morning we were told that we were under orders to join an entrenching battalion and that this twelfth of September would be our last day at the Base. It was a day of bustle during which we received many new instructions and counter-instructions, and spent much time going and coming from the Quartermaster's Stores. We had already felt sufficiently loaded, with our filled pack, rifle and heavy equipment, but to all this was now added a second gas helmet, a pair of tear-gas goggles, a day's rations and a supply of small-arms ammunition.

The draft throughout the day was patently in the grip of apprehension. The animal spirits never far below the surface failed to manifest themselves. We all had plenty of food for thought and it was perhaps as well that there was plenty to be done. During these days Jimmy and I had drawn closer together. We had been friendly at home, but there had been plenty of other distractions. Here under the new stresses, where in any case the tendency to pairing operated more strongly, we had begun to depend upon one another to defend mutual interests when apart and to refine our impressions when together.

This phenomenon of palship was a common experience of army life, varying in strength with the individuals. Some were so gregarious that they always consorted in groups, a few so individualistic as to maintain a degree of lonely isolation, but the majority hunted in pairs and although a somewhat shy character I certainly belonged to this category. The time had now arrived for us to exchange the addresses of our nearest relations and to promise each to write to them should anything happen.

This day could have been the hour of glory about which poets have been enraptured. Forebodings only filled our minds and the traditional light-heartedness of the Tommy had for the moment left us. Was I a coward? I do not know where the line between cowardice and fear is drawn; certainly I was filled with fear. During the months ahead fear was hardly ever to leave me and there were moments of terror. I do not believe this was unusual, though these are matters of our inner being not easily probed and perhaps only occasionally comprehended by others.

Thus on the night of 12th September 1916, my heart filled with dread, my mind filled with apprehensions of the unknown tomorrow and vague wishes that I might suddenly awaken from a bad dream only half begun, in reassuring proximity to those others who crowded the small tent, each man finding his own thoughts too precious just then to share with any one else, I stretched my feet under the blankets towards the centre pole and fell asleep.

III: TO THE FRONT

On the following morning reveille was at 2.00 a.m. and the camp was soon agog with preparations for departure. With half-opened eyes we dressed in haste, rolled and stacked our blankets, rushed for a hurried breakfast which was ready within the half hour and, just before 4.00 a.m. as the first grey shafts of the new day began to streak the sky, were bundled into waiting cattle trucks which bore the painted inscription 'Hommes 36, Chevaux 8'. This seemed crowded enough but in fact forty men or eight horses was the more usual standard, as we were later to discover. The trucks were dirty, draughty and comfortless. We had to squat or sprawl on the floor, using the various projections around the sides for hanging our rifles and equipments.

All day the train jogged northwards past drab hamlets and carefully cultivated but uninteresting, countryside. Our destination, which we reached in the early evening, proved to be Poperinghe, a small town not far from Ypres. I was immediately interested to discover that we had crossed from France into Belgium, only a small corner of which remained in Allied hands, but it was some days before I had figured out our proximity to the front long famed as 'the Salient'. That Poperinghe itself was the birthplace of the famous Talbot House, or Toc H Club, I did not know, nor do I remember that I became aware of this during my stay in the district.

Poperinghe was still trying to ignore its nearness to the line. It was a typical little Flanders town of the type that we had seen from the train, with cobbled streets and quaint little squares. Every street had its gaps, like extracted teeth, where enemy shells had exposed indecently the intimacies of some unfortunate family's home. Yet most of the other buildings seemed to be still occupied and the town was bustling with activity, doing its utmost to carry on business as usual. I looked about me with interest and was amazed that ordinary people could continue with the business of life in such close proximity to sudden death. It is true that I had already witnessed the dire results of Zeppelin bombing in London but the facts of war were still too unreal, compared with the normal security of life, to be accepted yet as a matter of course. As I gazed upon the rather phlegmatic and certainly unheroic-looking townsfolk proceeding about their normal routines, their apparent nonchalance impressed me beyond all else on that day of strange adventure.

I quickly became aware of an unexpected factor: the streets were abnormally filled with traffic, a traffic that flowed through the town in no haphazard manner. Intermixed with the jogging farm waggons, drawn by large brown horses, was a much larger contingent of army horse-drawn General Service waggons and mule-drawn limbers, with here and there a Red Cross motor ambulance or an Army Service Corps van. At the main crossings the traffic was being directed by khaki-clad policemen whose stolid businesslike demeanour indicated the training, and probably the actual experience, of the London 'Bobby'.

Our route took us through and beyond the town along one of those straight continental roads, sentinelled with trees, that never seem to end. Fortunately we were not seeking the end, which might well have landed us in enemy trenches, but turned off near the little village of Elverdinghe, along a cutting into a wood by a track which shortly brought us upon the camp that was our immediate destination. Here amidst the trees which sheltered it from enemy observation, were cunningly concealed the bivouacs of the 110th Entrenching Battalion, our new unit. All around, sheltered by the trees, were scores of squat dwellings built of logs and sandbags and roofed with tarpaulins.

The task of bundling us into groups and assigning us to these rather draughty, dirty tenements was soon effected in the falling dusk, and we were appalled at the number of bodies that authority assigned to each shelter, though we were soon to learn that being overcrowded had its compensations on a chilly night. In fact these 'bivvies' proved to be more tolerable habitations than first appearances had promised.

In the morning light of our first day there the camp looked much more attractive. The mysterious shadows of the previous night had departed with the dawn and the fading autumnal leaves formed a pleasant canopy over our heads, while the camp paths often led through open spaces that had a gladelike appearance. Despite occasional gas alarm points and warning notices which indicated the proximity of deadly war, we soon decided that we had landed in a pleasant enough place which had distinct attractions, compared say with our previous quarters at Etaples or even the moors of Harrogate. It is true that our liberty was restricted to a mile's radius in all directions but fortunately these territories included a Church Army hut which provided a comfortable rendezvous.

Our first day passed in the usual routines of kit inspection and the communication by petty authority of special instructions on discipline and emergencies such as air and gas attacks. It was a brief leisurely period of settling in. For the first time we received steel helmets. I found mine difficult to fit and uncomfortable to wear. It seemed to ride inconclusively on my head above the inner frame of rubber that cushioned it, but I was soon to get used to this peculiar headgear which always communicated a sense of security that was out of all proportion to its true protective capacities, considerable as these undoubtedly were.

The following morning we were awakened at a quarter to four and, lightly equipped for working party with rifle, bandolier of ammunition, haversack and steel and gas helmets, were on the road within the hour. This 15th September was a memorable date to me, as the day on which I first approached near to the German line, though it did little to modify the somewhat formalized picture in my mind of what the trenches would be like. Pictures of the front line had usually conveyed the impression of a narrow zigzagging cut in the ground, the sides neatly lined with sandbags and so deep that one could see over the top only by mounting the fire-step carved into the bays on the sides facing the enemy. At intervals along the trench, well below the level of the ground, were the entrances to the dugouts in which the troops dwelt when not on duty. In front of the trench line at a suitable distance there would be a regular belt of barbed wire to impede any enemy approach. Behind the front line were lines of support and reserve trenches which were linked to the forward and rear lines by deep communication trenches, along which supplies were carried and the relieving units travelled to the forward positions. This was the idealized picture of the battle zone instilled by the accounts I had read and the training I had received, but it was completed by notions of the sort of activity that I visualized as going on there.

In my mind there was something mystical about the place where our troops had close contact with the enemy and where death was the frequent arbiter. The men who served in such positions were most certainly not as other men were. Alive or dead they had already earned immortality and I could not, even at that late hour, imagine myself belonging to such a worthy company. That state, I thought, would in any case be gently reached by a sort of graduated approach whereby the novice was initiated into the mysteries necessary to make him an effective member of the elect. Only the most skilled would find a place in the front line, for it would have been fatal to allow the incompetent to become members of that company. This seemed to me to be the chief office of the support and reserve lines — to enable the tenderfoot to become acclimatized. Such was my personal picture, sufficiently near the truth to take the strain of reality as it was to unfold. I was undoubtedly fortunate to have this brief initial experience on a quiet front.

For a while we walked in single file along a railway track, finding the spacing of the sleepers uncomfortable for marching; then we joined the road and went forward directly towards the village of Boesinghe, or so at least the signposts indicated. We walked silently as we had been trained to do, but also from choice for this was an awesome experience, not merely to myself but, I feel sure, to most of the trudging band.

At first there was little to suggest that we were bound towards the enemy's positions. There were no guns firing, no rifle shots to be heard. Certainly the countryside had a deserted look, but to my unskilled eyes the abandoned grassy fields were just grazing lands. There was no one about except for an occasional nonchalant sentry in a little sandbagged shelter by the road. I did not envy him his job but he seemed to require none of my sympathy. Gradually the picture began to change. There were occasional shell holes in the fields, and trenches, now abandoned, traversing the countryside, came up to the road on either side, their protecting hedges of barbed wire looking neglected and forlorn, some iron pickets skewered down near the ground and all badly rusting.

There were shattered cottages and, more significant to us, wooden crosses scattered here and there usually near the road or by abandoned trenches. They gave the dead soldier's name, if it were known, and his regiment, and invariably bore the letters R.I.P. boldly painted. Sometimes a German soldier was similarly commemorated.

These grim reminders of the heavy fighting that had occurred on this front in 1915 were clearly being taken to heart by the quiet, expectant file of 'rookies' going forward for the first time to the line. We were so keyed up that, I feel certain, had something not shortly happened someone would have screamed.

The transformation came quickly as we approached the shattered, roofless, village of Boesinghe. White shell-bursts in the sky beyond the village indicated the approach of an enemy aeroplane reconnoitring in our direction. Our anti-aircraft batteries were opening up with staccato bursts as we entered the cleared open space in front of the church which was little more than a facade. The end of the nave was intact and surmounted by a crucifix that still pointed confidently to the sky. This sort of immunity of the symbol of Christianity had become a legend among the troops, and no doubt one's mind subconsciously picked out this kind of detail and remembered it. I can see the shape of that church wall still, though the rest of the scene is now lacking in precision.

Suddenly there was a rushing whining noise that seemed to be making straight towards us. Without more ado the file of men scattered and sprawled lovingly to the ground. I felt a cold shiver run down my spine as the shell thudded among the surrounding rubble not far away. Laconically the non-commissioned officer in charge of the party, who had not participated in the spontaneous scatter, affirmed that it was only an anti-aircraft dud. I felt a little foolish, but there was never anything foolish in being on the safe side, if that were possible. Thus we were to learn the ropes.

Our destination proved to be a massive chateau just outside the village, now occupied by the Royal Engineers and used as a store. It was approached by a gap in the high surrounding wall, still substantially intact. The building itself had scars from numerous bombardments but its shattered walls still indicated the fine proportions of its architecture, while the neglected grounds retained signs of the beauty that had once delighted its occupants. At the back of the building, away from the enemy line, there was still plenty of shelter from anything but the most aggressive shell-fire. The Royal Engineers at least seemed quite satisfied with their quarters. They could go down into their deep dugouts whenever there was serious gunfire. Our job that morning was to carry frames of wire netting, which the engineers had manufactured, to the reserve trench a few hundred yards away across the fields. These were for revetting the sides of the trench and preventing their crumbling and falling in, a job controlled by the Royal Engineers who depended upon the infantry to supply fatigue parties in aid of their more expert activities.

We arrived back in camp by midday much fatigued. No doubt the effect of our long walk and morning's labours had been magnified by the nervous tension naturally induced by a first journey to the trenches, although in fact it had been almost without incident and a far more mundane experience than I had anticipated. Now our ire was raised by an immediate order to prepare for inspection in full marching-order by the Colonel of the battalion. This meant, as usual, a hectic rush to clean rifles and adjust equipment, as well as to polish buckles and buttons. The latter operation astonished and annoyed me beyond words, for I had expected all this nonsense to be dropped as soon as we reached the fighting zone and found a serious job of work to do. It never was dropped, and I have no doubt that it served some purpose in keeping idle hands occupied, on the lines of the army's peacetime experience. None the less it never failed to annoy the rank and file who believed it made no contribution to winning the war and was designed only to rile them. When the Colonel did arrive, after we had been meticulously drawn up in review order, he paid every attention to our superficial cleanliness and none at all to us as human beings. It struck me then that the old regular officers in charge of such units were still living in a world of their own, a world of parades and rule books, that they were pampered figureheads with sycophantic aides and batmen, and had little sense of what was really happening around them. They treated us as they had learned to treat their peacetime soldiers, as automata made of different clay from themselves. They left the real job of work to the junior officers and NCOs while they masked their incompetence and ministered to their own pride by ensuring that the King's Regulations were strictly observed and their own authority never questioned. Though the officers were not all of this type, there were plenty of them, and the reactions of the troops, as I remember, were invariably scathing. If our leaders had had an inkling of the sentiments expressed about them none but the most hardened could have preserved any *amour propre*.

That evening, when our natural exasperation had all but disappeared, the sense of reasonable security that the camp had instilled was rudely shattered. Seventy members of our draft had been ordered to stand by to join our regiment in the line.

Fortunately neither Jimmy nor I was included but the immediate future assumed that threatening, unsettled appearance that it had had for us at the base. One could never know what the morrow would bring forth. Looking back with aftersight one can now realise that this situation was a peculiar repercussion of battles like the Somme whose continuing pressures for more and more human fodder put all other arrangements out of joint.

As it turned out, the following day was to be more eventful in a double sense. We set off again on the same errand. On our way along the railway track my ingrained collector's proclivities were excited by the sight of a complete fern-shape in one of the pieces of shale with which the track had been built up. Although not large it was a fairly heavy piece to carry in my haversack. When I got back to camp I tried to pare away some of the surplus fringe but, to my chagrin, it broke right across the fossilized pattern and that was an end to it, which was perhaps just as well as I should have been mad to attempt to carry such a heavy souvenir around with me. There was a standing order against our adding to our already heavy load, but this was largely negatived by a general tendency to collect souvenirs and even to 'win' things before they were lost. The real prizes were German spiked helmets (*Pickelhauben*) or revolvers, though almost any portable piece of enemy equipment would do. Our ASC motor drivers were the most inveterate and successful of these souvenir hunters, for they not only had the means of transport at their disposal but their tradesmen's rates of pay enabled them to pay highest prices. They had little chance of acquiring anything at first hand.

One popular line of collecting which I had noticed from the very outset manifested itself in the embellishment of web belts with cap badges, both British and foreign, acquired during the owner's journeyings. The oldest soldiers almost invariably sported belts weighty with many months' accumulation of this rather innocuous form of scalp-hunting. In the same way holiday travellers affix labels on their luggage or plaques on their walking sticks as emblems of their halting places.

That day, while we were working in the same trench, the enemy bombarded a position a hundred yards or so away. For the first time I heard heavy shells grumbling over at, seemingly, a leisurely pace, bursting with a heavy thud and throwing up a black fountain of smoke and debris; some fell in our vicinity. I experienced an odd shiver as I instinctively flattened myself to the trench side, but the feeling soon passed as it became clear that the shells were not intended for us, and I made only a tentative gesture of self-effacement. I remarked how quickly one became adjusted to a new and rather fearful experience and could not refrain from wondering how I should react when I found myself in a target area.

Although the front had awakened only for a short period on this day its possibilities were already much plainer than they had been the day before, and I did not feel that future working parties would be any more attractive. I was not therefore upset when, on my return to camp, I was ordered to report immediately to the Company Quarter Master Sergeant who, in scanning the paybooks, had discovered that I was qualified for the job of company clerk. He offered me the post and, at the mere thought of thus missing the working parties, I accepted with alacrity. But before the end of the day I was beginning to question the wisdom of my choice. I had been kept hard at work until it was time to go to bed and then I was not happy to discover that I was expected to sleep alone in the orderly tent away from the rest of the draft.

My new chief was amiable enough, an insurance clerk in civil life, holding the rank of full corporal and hoping to obtain full warrant rank on his new job. During the short while I was with him I learned that he wanted more than anything in the world to hang on to his new post which was in process of building up, doubtless with the assistance of others higher up whose minds were working in the same direction. I was to be part of his means to this end. For myself I had no wider objective than to miss the working parties, and I was not even greatly concerned about that. I was merely taking the line of least resistance. It never occurred to me then or later that there were any cards worth playing. I did not want to be killed but I did not consider any plan to render the possibility less likely. I did not want clerical work in the army — in fact I always inwardly despised army clerks — and this was to be the only time while the fighting lasted that I found myself on work of that type. I had joined up to be a fighting soldier and a fighting soldier I would remain until the job was over. Then I would leave it all without delay. A similarly unenterprising attitude coupled with a somewhat modest assessment of my own leadership capacities — for I only went to a secondary school in which the masters were all grossly overworked — was to prevent my bothering about promotion in the ranks.

On the following day my morale received a grievous shock. While scanning battalion orders I came across an entry announcing that the sentence of such and such a court martial had been duly carried out that morning. My curiosity aroused, further delving into the file brought to light the fact that a certain Private had recently been taken into custody at Hazebrouck as a deserter and sentenced by General Field Court Martial to death.

This opened up to me a hidden facet of the glory of war about which I had not previously thought. It was a blow to both my sense of honour and my sense of proportion. While I had no excuse to offer for the delinquent and it was sad to reflect upon his weakness, it was a fearful shock to learn that death could be considered the appropriate penalty. I discovered that the camp records were punctuated with announcements of this sort. In subsequent discussion with the Quartermaster Sergeant, who seemed to have steeped himself in this sort of lore, I gathered that these terrible reprisals were reported to fond parents as 'killed in action'; somehow that very proper procedure made the whole matter even more abhorrent to me.

Looking back today, it is not easy for me to appreciate the outrageous shock that that laconically worded official notice had upon my innocence. My youthful idealism had received a blow from which it would never recover; but there were others to follow.

Very soon we learned of our own imminent departure to join our proper regiment and I had to face up to the early prospect of losing my somewhat privileged position. Our camp, despite its inconsequences and niggling annoyances, suddenly became a most attractive place. The annoyances were many and multifarious. On the first rainy night the inconveniences of dwelling in flooded bivouacs under dripping trees were quickly manifest. To them was added the fear that the rain would continue, as well it could in Flanders, and that a projected trip to Poperinghe on the passes I had negotiated would be prevented. But the rain did stop and Jimmy and I had our evening out.

One afternoon I was crossing the camp on an errand when I passed the Regimental Sergeant-Major looking very resplendent, as they often did. I saluted him automatically and earned a public telling off for my pains. First-class warrant officers were not entitled to this acknowledgement but they could wear a Sam Browne and a uniform of officer's cut and their sleeve insignia of the Royal Arms was not always clear at a distance. Such a mistake might be excusable when one encountered such a well-turned-out example, but it was none the less militarily quite deplorable. I deplored it myself. It would not have mattered so much had the incident ended there but not long after, when on a similar errand, I passed an officer some distance away. Feeling that he too might be a sergeant-major but was in any case out of reasonable range on this occasion I withheld my tribute. A message arrived at our office post-haste that the new clerk should be reminded of his military duties and reprimanded. I felt very small, but this self-condemnation did not prevent my considering the entire business childish and unnecessarily irritating.

That same night, as I lay in my office, I heard shells travelling overhead towards Poperinghe and I tried to imagine the kind of havoc they were causing among the dwellers in that steadfast place. My admiration for those Belgians was unstinted, yet I could not understand why they stayed in danger when safety could be sought without breaking any code. Some, I knew, had stayed because it was profitable to meet the soldiers' needs. While the larger shops, often shattered, had closed down, smaller ones in deserted houses had sprung up all over the place to sell those small things that every soldier needed, particularly cleaning materials, chocolate, cigarettes and light refreshments. Had I thought a little more deeply I should have recollected that to all of them this was still 'home'.

We had already had a pay parade at which we each received five francs, a sum then sufficient to keep us solvent. At the same time there had been a free issue of cigarettes, a brand known as Flag, which was one of the special varieties produced for the troops. This was a welcome occasion to the smokers, and now began a routine which always gave me a special call upon popularity during my service abroad. As a non-smoker I could bestow my issue on someone else and Jimmy was naturally the happy recipient. I never failed to be surprised both at the joy of the smoker who had a good supply of the weed and at the unquestionable agony of the genuineness and strength of their reactions. Fortunately I was never the least tempted; perhaps my resolution had been tempered by the gloating prophesy of a friend still in civilians, who on receiving the news of my enlistment had predicted that now I would surely acquire the habit.

In a batch of papers that arrived on the day before our departure we read some amazing news and our hopes for an early ending to the struggle were buoyed up beyond measure. It is a strange thing that throughout that first great upheaval there persisted from the very beginning a general tendency to believe, on the flimsiest evidence, that the war would come to a sudden end.

Now we had a tangible basis for our inveterate optimism. During the continuing battle of the Somme, in the capture of a place called Flers, a weird armoured contraption had appeared on the battlefield in support of our attacking troops. It ran on moving tractors, carried machine-guns and was called a 'tank'. The pictures in the papers showed a funny elliptical shape up-ended at the front, and I thought at once of H. G. Wells's inventive fantasies. Impervious to rifle and machine-gun fire, to hand grenades and shrapnel, this armoured vehicle had crossed the barbed wire over the enemy trenches and roamed along the back of the line shooting down every head raised above the ground.

We were elated, and filled with enthusiasm that our side had produced this surprise. There was much mirth over the ridiculous reactions of the enemy when faced by this unconquerable monstrosity. How much there was of wishful thinking in these understandable reactions!

The remainder of this day was again spent in the usual desultory preparations which left plenty of time for dwelling upon our fears of the unknown future. Another routine medical inspection confirmed, more or less, our fitness to depart. Iron rations, only to be used in emergency, were issued in the form of a one-pound tin of bully beef, a small tin of tea and sugar, and some hard biscuits, all tied up in a white cloth bag. At the same time we were cautioned about the dire penalties that would follow any breaking into these unappetising foodstuffs without prior instructions.

Swearing and talk that was often dirty, sometimes blasphemous were common habit in the army and most of us wasted much breath on unnecessary expletives. That morning, keyed up no doubt by the tension of our preparations, two members of the draft came to blows after one had called the other 'a bastard'. It was an army convention that this word was taboo on the grounds that it insulted not only the recipient but his mother. Prevailing public opinion decreed that such a lapse could be repaired only by apology or a fight. Even an NCO or officer could be called to account for its use. This particular fight, a somewhat haphazard encounter, for neither of the protagonists were pugilistic, was eventually stopped by the bystanders.

That evening Jimmy and I found our way to the Church Army canteen to make merry, or as merry as our heavy hearts would permit. I tried to drink some of the innocuous native beer but, despite its anaemic content, found it unpalatable, as beer has always remained to me. At the closure we were joined by Corry and Matthews, both under twenty like ourselves. We talked inevitably of home, touched upon our apprehensions about the front, wherever it might be, opining that where we were was very quiet and no criterion of what it would be like elsewhere. In an excess of nostalgia and half-hope we made a compact that, should we four survive till Christmas, a similar celebration should be arranged. Fate was not to be kind to this apparently reasonable assignation. One was to be dead, a second a casualty, a third still active, while the fate of the fourth I do not remember.

Thus it was that on 21st September 1916 my journey up to the real firing line began. We expected to reach the Somme but hoped against hope that our destination might be somewhere else. The draft entrained during the morning at Poperinghe in cattle trucks but this time we were not overcrowded. In our truck there was a contingent of a Yorkshire Regiment returning after a spell away from the line as casualties. At the outset there was an indefinable barrier between the two groups. As beings who had already had an experience that we both feared and half-envied, we treated them with respect.

All day the train jogged along, stopping at all stations and almost everywhere else, as it seemed, on the smallest provocation. The weather was fine and with the sliding doors full open we sat for a time with our feet dangling over the line, watching fruitful but monotonous countryside gradually slipping by. Tired at last of seeing little and doing nothing we returned to our packs to read or play cards, and between whiles we made tea with water from the engine which we scrounged at halts.

It was towards evening that the train crawled into Calais with its uninteresting rows of drab red-brick houses. Naturally our thoughts turned to the comparative proximity of England, and the songs and laughter died away. We were shunted into a siding for the night, and a most uncomfortable night it was. The truck, with its hard floor and no blankets to ward off the cold draughts, had certainly not been designed as a bedroom even under the most favourable conditions. In the morning bare rations were issued. Fortunately we were able to supplement them at a canteen and Salvation Army hut which we had found nearby. It is surprising how much and how frequently one can eat when there is nothing much to do. And most of us were young.

The second day of our journey saw a definite thawing between the two groups and our Yorkshire comrades proved to be very cheery fellows. We tried with little success to draw them out about the line which they habitually treated as a joke. One said laconically, 'Don't ask, you'll soon know. It's just hell.' Snatches of conversation among themselves were far from reassuring. 'Poor old Mac, killed up at Ploegstreet.' 'Young Jones badly smashed in the April do.' Such remarks needed no verbal embroidery.

During the afternoon the temperature had risen and the sun shone invitingly through the open door. Our companions, who had already shown numerous signs of bodily discomfort, were glad of the opportunity to take off their shirts and hunt out the 'chats', the polite army term for human body lice. We were shown, for the first time, some particularly bloated specimens of these loathsome vermin, gorged to the full with the blood of their protesting host. It was pointed out that the black marking on their backs resembled an iron-cross. So far I had not experienced this minor annoyance of life at the front but it was a plague from which no one at that time could hope to escape. Even officers, whose facilities for a change of clothing and personal cleansing were so much superior to ours, were unable to keep free under the conditions of the line.

It was in the middle of the afternoon that we reached Abbeville, a thriving base crammed with troops and military dumps. We were given no clue to the probable duration of our stay, but the opportunity to stretch our legs was not to be missed. Jimmy and I decided to risk a foray as far as the YMCA hut for refreshments. There a notice board announced an evening show by the Lena Ashwell Concert Party, which included prominent performers from the music halls who were devoting their services to the amusement of the troops at the front. Places like Abbeville, situated well back at the mouth of the Somme, were 'the front' to most of those who came from Britain and it was to the base wallahs and such itinerants as ourselves that shows of this sort were most frequently given. This surely was not an opportunity to be missed. As there were still no signs of movement or any definite embargo to confine us to the train we slipped away during the evening to enjoy the entertainment by the famous troupe. The hut was filled to overflowing with a highly appreciative and participative audience who joined vociferously in those wartime songs which evoked an enthusiastic response unequalled by any since. Strategically placed at the back of the hall we were a bit apprehensive about the train and, not uninfluenced perhaps by fears of the penalties of desertion, we slipped away at 9.30 p.m. while the singing was in full spate, fortunately, for, the train began to move without warning just as we arrived.

Our second night on the train was even less comfortable than the first since movement increased the draughts, but I slept more for I was now very tired. When we slid back the doors the next morning the countryside had considerably changed. Bathed in the morning sun was a pleasant rolling landscape with green fields and shady lanes. It all had a much more homely look. We were penetrating, though we were still unaware of the fact, the fruitful pasture lands of the valley of the Somme. Now and again we passed groups of French soldiers on the march, different branches in varying shades of the light blue which they were then wearing, interspersed now and again with khaki-clad Turcos from Africa with their red fezes. At one place we passed large squads of German prisoners in greenish grey, working apparently with a will and not unhappy in their fate. Obviously they did not envy us our freedom and I could not resist reflecting upon the irony of our different situations.

Our jog-trot journey continued all day. We seemed to be making a wide detour but veering back in the direction of the line. During the evening an enemy plane, flying high over the train, seemed to threaten something drastic but our driver continued onwards unconcernedly and shortly the intruder gave way before the high bursting anti-aircraft shells that were flecking the lovely blue above us. At last, at 8.30 p.m., we steamed into the station of Albert. Alongside the railway a heavy battery was firing with demoniac energy and I had my first sight of guns in action. The noise of each discharge was shattering. The flashes from the recoiling guns seemed literally to envelop us as we left the train. Between each discharge the gunners glided about the guns like automata, so that it was difficult to believe in their humanity. None of us was sorry when the order came to move off.

We filed through the shattered town of Albert, the great supply centre behind the battle lines of the Somme, a place we were to become more closely acquainted with in the months ahead. It appeared, even on first sight a characterless sort of place and I had little reason later to change my opinion. What surprised me was the great amount of activity that was obviously going on there, despite the severe damage evident on all sides. We crossed the open place by the damaged cathedral, of nondescript style, constructed of brickwork with cornices of stone. Its battered tower was capped by an immense effigy of the Virgin and Child now bent down perilously from its base towards the road. Its fall seemed imminent, indeed certain at the very next hit. Our guide told us current legend had it that its fall would denote the end of the war. I learned later that the Royal Engineers had strongly secured it in its present position.

We left the cobbled streets and straight house-fronts behind and marched out into the gathering gloom. The night was clear and stars were beginning to appear in the sky. I felt an indefinable strangeness, not without foreboding, as I looked towards the darkening horizon ahead. Beyond this was our destination, and what else? I shuddered as I remembered the demoniac fury of the heavy guns near the station and the deathly shadows that had clung to the gaunt broken walls of the shattered houses of Albert. There surely the realm of death began. Yet all around was so quiet and still and, in the uniform cloak of gloom that had now gathered over the land, seemingly undisturbed by man's contrariness.

Presently as our feet began to tire we appeared to be entering a new zone. On either side of the long straight road numerous camp-fires began to twinkle and the feeling of serenity was even strengthened. The star-flecked expanse of land and sky created a weird impression. For a brief moment I had the feeling, which comes to one at such times when a new experience takes hold, that this new world was the real world in which a different me had been all the time, and found myself wondering why I had ever identified myself with one Norman Gladden who had dwelt in a different universe. In my present otherness I seemed destined to march throughout eternity towards the stars.

The unearthly feeling faded as we slithered to the welcoming grass by the side of the road. The halt, so very welcome, accentuated our fatigue. Our guide was vague about our destination. He seemed by no means certain that he would find the battalion where he had left it only a few hours before. We marched on again. A new note entered our surroundings. The rim of the horizon began to glimmer with even brighter lights, dancing up and down, as it seemed, but in fact mainly ascending as the enemy sent up his rockets like Roman candles to light the ground between the trenches. And there were longer flashes in the distant skies, while from nearby, amidst the fires, we began to see the flashes and hear the reports of discharging guns. The whole scene was being progressively lashed to a crescendo of lightnings and noise, a veritable inferno, incredible after its peaceful beginnings. In truth it had been the quiet prelude of the night that had been the illusion and this new spectacle of frightening, uncontrollable activity was the reality.

At last, when fear and fatigue were beginning to gain ascendancy, our guide announced that we had arrived and led us off the road, across broken ground into the waggon-lines of our new unit. Grim spectral shapes of horses moved uneasily about their posts. Here and there a few tents marked the sleeping places of the denizens of these lines; here and there the red glow of a camp-fire broke the nearer darkness. There was no one to receive the new draft. Our guide disappeared. Our own NCOs were as bewildered as the rest of us. For a moment resentment overcame fatigue. But standing in the cold, abandoned and still expecting someone in authority to do something for us we were in a particularly helpless position. The cold soon got the upper hand.

Jimmy and I tried to huddle together on the ground in our greatcoats, but the intermittent crashes of the neighbouring batteries banished all possibility of sleep. We stumped around or huddled up to one of the fires. Who the watchers round the fires were we did not know. No one spoke to us. Presumably they were on duty, otherwise there was no reason why they should have been out in the open in the middle of the night. They spoke in a dialect which sounded like Scots, but which I was soon to recognize as Tyneside, and even to speak myself. It was difficult at times to follow the ruminations of these old hands, who appeared at least to take our presence for granted and paid no special attention to us. They reminisced and talked of home with a sad longing in their voices and at least one of us felt near to tears.

But there were other, nearer themes, of women and beer and battle lines. One story, probably devised for present company though there was not the least indication of this at the time, told of the sad fate of the cooks of another battalion who had lit a fire and brought to it all the broken wood they could lay their hands on. It was a splendid, comforting blaze and the assembled group enjoyed their 'crack' (conversation). The ground grew hotter and hotter. Unfortunately the fire had been sited over a buried dud shell. And that was that. Jimmy and I edged away a little and I found myself working out the probable range of the heat-induced explosion of a shell buried in the ground. My estimate took me well beyond the range of the present welcoming heat.

I decided that to walk up and down at a safe distance would be an equally effective way of keeping warm. So through the cold night we alternately walked and huddled even after the firing batteries had desisted, and the weary sleepless hours gradually passed. In misery we watched the break of day as, for the first time for us, the sun rose to illuminate the battlefield of the Somme.

IV: THE CAPTURE OF LE SARS

When day broke after our first uncomfortable night on the Somme the scene before us was much different from what the darkness had promised. Instead of a barren landscape bristling with gun-pits, the rolling countryside in all directions teemed with life. A regular quilt of enclosures, tents, horse-lines, guns stretched to the horizon where a fringe of broken trees framed a scene that looked like some vast horse-fair. No permanent structure was to be seen, for the tide of battle which had but recently flowed across these fields had obliterated most standing objects. Here and there a few stark tree trunks marked the site of a once pleasant copse, here and there an aimless heap of broken red bricks marked the site of some erstwhile happy hamlet. Alongside the road not far away a large wooden board was labelled in bold letters Fricourt, the name of a village now reduced to a shapeless pile of rubble.

This was the supply area that moved with the tide of battle at a discreet distance behind the front line, out of reach of any but the longest range guns. Here were the shell dumps and stores, needed in unending supply to feed the greedy appetite of battle. Here were the heavy batteries, the general supply services and the transport units of the battalions in the line. Occasionally these areas were shelled. We were told that a day or two before our arrival this camp had been bombarded and a number of horses killed. In the main, however, there was little molestation and no serious effort was at that time made to hide the intensive activity of these rear zones from the eyes of the enemy. The menace from the air had not yet developed sufficiently to interfere materially with the hectic activities on which the holding of the battle-line so vitally depended. It was in this area that the captive balloons were usually moored and employed to keep a continuous watch upon the movements behind the enemy lines, especially to spot targets for the artillery. Strangely enough I did not take special note of these ungainly monsters at the time and do not remember seeing them on the Somme, though I feel sure that they were there.

It took me some time to sort out the detail of this scene of remarkable activity. A most welcome sight in the foreground was the field kitchen in full blast, but, we were shocked to discover, not for us as no rations had yet been issued for the new draft. We had to scrounge, and a few scraps of bacon and some hard biscuits given grudgingly were all we could obtain. Our new unit, the 7th battalion of the Northumberland Fusiliers, in the 50th Territorial Division, certainly had a disconcertingly offhand way of welcoming its new members. We were soon to discover that our reception was not exceptional in this respect.

To be treated thus after such a night was beyond the limit, and it would be difficult to imagine a more depressed and disconsolate crowd than the draft on that late September morning. I felt that if there was a Purgatory this was surely it. We knew that there was worse to follow in the hell of actual battle, but that was unavoidable, while the present discomfort suggested a callousness that was barely credible and boded ill for the future. It is much easier to understand and condone in retrospect. In those days modern ideas of public relations and welfare had not yet developed and had they existed it is doubtful whether the military mind of the age, still used to viewing the common soldier in Kipling's pattern, would have paid any attention. The development of the Somme battle, now nearly three months old, had called for feats of co-ordination and organization with which the men on the spot had hardly been trained to cope. Improvisation was the order of the day. When we arrived the battalion was in the trenches; we were to wait with the transport until they came out. Obviously we were in the way and no one in authority was at the moment interested in our whereabouts.

During the morning something was done to provide us with shelter. By stretching an immense tarpaulin over a row of barbed-wire pickets, of which there were plenty available, and pegging it down at the two sides with wooden stakes we managed to improvise a low shelter. This might be some protection from the elements but evidently not from the infernal racket of artillery which was my intensest immediate worry. As a child I had always been very susceptible to sudden bangs, which literally made me jump. My fear now was that close proximity to artillery discharges would disclose to all around me how frightened of noise I was. Experience was soon to teach me that the nervous system is capable of coping with much worse stresses.

There did seem to me to be malicious intent in choosing for the site of our bivouac a spot seventy yards or so in front of 'Clara', a large eight-inch howitzer, scarred with gashes from counter shell-fire and obviously a veteran of the early stages of the great battle. When it fired, its stumpy barrel pointing skywards and belching immense shells into the air with a searing blast of flame, our tarpaulin lifted and flapped back disconcertingly as the air rushed into the semi-vacuum. I soon understood the commands issued to the gun team and sat keyed up for the next discharge as the order to fire was given. It was only the firmest resolution that prevented my throwing discretion to the winds and running away. Fortunately gunners get tired and howitzer shells are expensive, though there certainly seemed to be no shortage in the camouflaged stacks about the guns. Clara had plenty of time off from her death's work.

Later when we had found our feet, as it were, we fell into the habit of standing behind the gun when it was firing and by concentrated watching were able to pick up the black dot of the shell as it hurtled high towards the horizon and the enemy's positions. This was the only circumstances in which a launched shell could be seen — until it burst, of course. On such occasions the scene behind this vicious-looking gun, so charmingly nicknamed, was one of extreme purposefulness. We were fascinated by the display of energy on the part of the crew, whose members clearly had a great pride in, a sort of love for, their awful Clara, something indeed beyond the regard that any infantryman could have in the offensive means at his disposal. We at least could applaud the freedom with which Clara sent her donations to the enemy, for whom, certainly at this distance, we had no fellow-feeling. He deserved all he was getting.

After completing our afternoon task, a profitless effort with primitive means to clean harness, which had surely been set to keep us from too much idleness, Jimmy and I went in search of the mythical canteen, which reason must have hinted would have been sold out had we ever found it. This we never did, but instead, that afternoon, we stumbled across the old front line where the epic opening battle of 1st July had taken place. I do not think many of the details of the newspaper reports had stayed in our minds. They had certainly all been couched in too similar a key of optimism for any clear picture of the truth to have emerged. We had not then known that the casualties of the first few days had amounted to sixty thousand, but what we did see now was sufficient, with a little imagination, to convey to us something of what had been done and endured by those whom history had honoured by selecting them as participants in that epic but disappointing occasion.

We were looking down into what had evidently been the German front line, a system of trenches zigzagging through the white chalk that gashed the surface of the ground, cluttered with layers of sandbags disarrayed and broken by the fire from our artillery. A strong belt of wire had been cut in the same devastating storm, although sufficient must have remained to slow down the attackers. The earth all around had been churned up into shell holes, with here and there larger mine craters whose crumbling sides had been stained a greenish yellow by the explosions.

Unexploded shells and rotting equipment littering the ground, with here and there groups of wooden crosses, composed a picture which still conveyed a vivid idea of the grim struggle that had taken place on these once pleasant downs. Hereabouts the crosses of the British dead related mainly to members of a Yorkshire regiment, the particulars from the identity discs (which we all wore suspended about our necks) of the fallen having been transferred to the bare wood. Sometimes there were no details, and this was usually the case with the enemy dead who were assigned to their own little burial sectors. At this sad moment we could find no personal hatred for the numerous unknown German soldiers who must have sold their lives dearly in the conflict. Crossing this hallowed ground was like entering a church: I was both awed and horrified by what I saw and my fears for the future were accentuated by this vision of the recent past. I could not imagine myself living up to such an example, while my pity for those who would never again see the sunshine was overwhelming.

We wandered round in silence. Devastating as was this picture of reality, about which we had previously read so much but were only now actually beginning to comprehend for the first time, some measure of clearing up had already been carried out by our pioneer corps and the surrounding landscape was now too populated to present anything approximating its scene on that July morning.

In the broken trench line there were a number of dug-out entrances, their openings still encumbered with debris and marked with warning notices to the effect that closer investigation might prove dangerous; bombs, booby traps and unexploded mines were possible. From one of the gaping shafts there rose the sickly stench that we were to come to know so well. Unburied German bodies still lay where an attacker's bomb thrown down the stairway had killed all who had not already rushed up to surrender. Our curiosity sufficiently satisfied, we returned silently to camp.

That evening, Clara being silent, I sat under the flap of our low shelter engaged upon one of the dearest pastimes of the Tommy on foreign soil — writing home. There was so much to tell and the ever-present feeling that one's poorly scrawled message was the one direct contact with the only life that one now cared about, a life already become a fairy-tale to those who were on the brink of death. But censorship was always in attendance, the unhallowed eye of the duty officer who would read what I wrote, and in consequence the things I wrote were never more than formal messages of the type that were then streaming into England from all corners of the globe, from men whose hearts were keyed to the point of breaking. On the other hand, high art of description, of poetry itself, would have been needed to convey to those at home the barely coherent thoughts and impressions of a young man undergoing an ordeal for which his first nineteen years had provided little preparation. Even without the misty presence of the censor at my elbow, I am sure that the self-conscious literacy achieved by a good secondary school education such as the times provided, would have been inadequate to cope with such a shattering mental and spiritual experience.

In the evening the numerous shanties, bivouacs and horse-lines, peacefully ignoring the silent artillery, presented to my eye a picture of homely domesticity and made it difficult to visualize the reason for all these purposeful dispositions. A little way from where I sat there was a bell-tent occupied by officers of a signal unit. They had a small gramophone, wheezy as they all were at the time, and as I sat musing my ear picked up the refrain:

If you were the only girl in the world
And I were the only boy....

and my mind went back to a visit to the Alhambra in Leicester Square, to the 'Bing Boys Are Here', with George Robey and Violet Loraine singing that tuneful duet, and a wave of homesickness overwhelmed me. Whenever I hear the refrain — not one that is usually repeated with all the other popular songs of the trenches — I see that evening landscape on the Somme and my heart seems to falter with a pain that has never properly healed. If on that fine evening my feelings of nostalgia were directed to the terrace house in Putney, today when I hear the tune my thoughts travel in reverse across the years to those who suffered and died for ideals, that now seem based upon some indefinable illusion.

Our battalion had come out of the trenches into what was known as reserve. We were ordered to join them in their new position and my military education proceeded apace. Marching along the finely engineered main road, past innumerable camps and transports, we mounted a slight incline and entered the less populated areas of the smaller heavies — mainly sixty-pounders — which literally fringed the road. They were in action. Enemy shells in reply were throwing up black fountains of earth and smoke on the ridge, and I sensed something of the fear that I knew closer experience would intensify. Yet it was difficult, even after all we had seen, to realise the essence of the terror which was now at hand.

The ridge was crowned by the gaunt remains of two woods, one on each flank. We left the road along a path which led to a cutting into the wood on the right, and we were not sorry to be thus veering away from the spot that the enemy were shelling. We had hardly started on this new route when we passed a straggling party of dishevelled soldiers, among whom we recognized members of the first draft which had left us at Elverdinghe. They were now attached to the 4th Battalion of our regiment and had a doleful tale to tell, very abruptly as we went by. On their very first working party they had been shelled and half the draft had become casualties. Thus many of those whom we had known at Harrogate had already perished. Such brief battle experience was the not uncommon lot of reinforcements from home.

Depressed by this news and the unkempt appearance of our erstwhile companions, we continued through the cutting to an open space where the trees formed a rough V which, we were told, was the billet of our new battalion. This was Mametz Wood where there had been heavy fighting. An old trench with dug-outs, a tent and a few bivouacs were all that we could see in the shape of habitations. The ground all around was seared and torn by shell-fire and encumbered with all sorts of debris.

A few solitary figures walking amidst this desolation were hardly recognizable as soldiers.

Again there was no reception committee. We were shared out among the four companies, one small batch, which included Jimmy and myself, being assigned to C Company. We were then left without further ceremony to fend for ourselves. All the dug-outs appeared to be full and our tentative approaches were met by scowling looks or faces that seemed too weary even to scowl. A more ill-assorted, bad-humoured-looking crowd would be difficult to imagine, with not a single word of welcome among them. No doubt the men were too concerned with their recent ordeal and present discomforts to bother about a few newcomers who had been enjoying themselves at home, but this hardly excused the officers. We noticed that a few earlier unfortunates had made bivvies for themselves and decided that there was nothing to do but follow their example. And this we did after consuming a microscopic ration of tea that was shortly issued from the field kitchen parked near the trench.

Necessity in that unreal world was most certainly the mother of invention. Jimmy and I selected a suitably shaped shell-hole, which had not been polluted with garbage, and dug off from it a ledge long and wide enough for us to sleep upon side by side. Our two groundsheets were then tied and propped up to make a covering with the outer edges buried in the ground. Entering our improvised shelter from the end where it ran into the shell-hole, we lay huddled side by side for warmth with our feet towards the opening. We slept in our great-coats on a layer of newspapers which was all that protected us from the damp ground. Sleep came fitfully for the night was cold and moisture soon began to rise from the soil.

I was not sorry to be moving about and eating my breakfast of a scoop of tea in my mess-tin lid and a shrivelled piece of bacon on a diminutive piece of bread that I had managed to dip in the fat at the bottom of the dixie in which it had been served at the cook-house. We paraded at 7.00 a.m. for working party.

Our unprepossessing companions accepted our presence with no show of interest, as though this sort of thing had been going on so regularly that they took it for granted. They saw newcomers merely as more mouths to share rations, which were already too short for young men living in such conditions. Our job on this day, at a cross-roads not far away, consisted in breaking stones and levelling out the road with pick, shovel and broom. All was quiet and the weather was fine. Troops of all branches and many different infantry units passed back and forth all the time. There were cheery hails between those who recognized an acquaintance, but mainly they were silent groups. One heard just the pad of their feet and the clanking of entrenching tools.

I looked in vain for those laughing faces so often featured in the papers at home, and remembered wryly the journalists' tales of enthusiastic troops eager to get at the Hun. Such manifestations would have been incredible in the particular circumstances. In their imaginative pictures, the writers had failed to interpret the underlying truth. I soon became terribly bored; the work left me too much energy for thought. Fears began to crowd uncontrolled into my imagination, and I was not sorry when at last we were fallen in and led back to camp.

It was now 4.00 p.m. We had our first ration issue. A broken loaf was to be shared among ten of us, a tin of jam and some butter among every seven men; a tin of biscuits, hard and broken, was opened and stood by the company tent. It was immediately raided as by a pack of wolves and emptied. We found it difficult to lay hands on our rations: their guardians, when discovered in the derelict trenches, handed them over reluctantly as though granting a great favour. I doubted the right of my exiguous bread ration to the claim of being anything like a tenth of a loaf, but I was too raw yet to make any protest. The only other addition to this meagre diet was the somewhat flavourless bully-beef stew dished out at the kitchen soon after our return. We used our mess-tins for this and had somehow to keep them clean with cold water at a water-point set up at the edge of the wood.

Our second day was again a quiet one. In the morning we were marched in search of a bath but were disappointed. On reaching the makeshift canvas enclosures covering the bathing plant which had been established amid the horse lines in the back areas, it was discovered that the baths were out of order. This was a serious deprivation for the arrangements for washing on the Somme were primitive to say the least. In the back and reserve areas there were water-points and stand-pipes but further forward, as I was to learn later, water had to be taken up in petrol cans and dumped. It usually tasted of petrol as well as chloride of lime, the latter added for health reasons, and was often completely undrinkable. Naturally, in the circumstances a scarce commodity like water was not to be squandered for washing purposes, except by officers' batmen who seemed to spend much of their time, even when in the line, in keeping their charges spick and span, so that the latter invariably appeared at their best, like Hollywood film actors.

The rest of the day was spent in being inspected. First it was our ammunition, which we were admonished to keep dry and clean; then it was our feet which the Medical Officer's orderly surveyed for signs of trench feet, an incapacity similar to frostbite that had until recently been treated as a crime. Finally the Colonel came along with all the usual ceremony to inspect the new draft. He was a regular soldier, important in manner, severe if slightly wooden in mien. He comported himself with the accepted parade-ground demeanour which struck me as out of place in such surroundings. There was no friendliness, no apparent interest in us; we were looked at as a horse and trap might have been looked at, though with less sympathy. What he thought of us could be guessed and I hardly blamed him. Our reactions to him had they been made manifest would have merited a firing party.

That night the heavens took a hand. It rained, and our flimsy covering was washed in upon us. Fortunately the downpour did not persist, but it was not possible to re-erect our bivouac in the sodden earth. The clammy blackness of the night was lightened by a first ray of friendliness. Two fellow sufferers in a neighbouring shell-hole, more enterprising than ourselves, lit a fire which they invited us to share. This we did with alacrity and no little pleasure, and we made the acquaintance of Bryant and Taylor, two Yorkshiremen who had joined the battalion but a few weeks earlier. While we dried our garments by the welcome blaze fed by the broken wood that abounded, they told us of their experiences, which sadly confirmed all our worst fears about our new unit whose staff and men considered every new draft fair game for the filching of privileges. We were told that we should have to learn the ropes and take a hand in the constant struggle of all against each. We completed the night in front of the dying embers, sitting up with our backs propped against the earthy sides of the shell-hole, huddled as closely as we could and doing our utmost to shelter our faces from the chill night breeze that blew out of the surrounding darkness. I was both hot and cold, on opposite sides.

The next morning I felt so ill and was suffering from the symptoms of diarrhoea common in the camp that I decided I had to go sick. This was an important decision on my part since it was the first time since I joined up that I had reported to a Medical Officer. I had little use for the man, not by any means uncommon in the ranks, who went sick for the smallest ailment or indeed for none at all. Perhaps it was not fair to blame the MO for his habitual reaction, which was to treat all his clients as 'lead swingers', as we called them. Those clients were mainly of the one type and he seemed to have little understanding of the majority whom he rarely saw, except as participants in a mass inspection.

I received no sympathy that morning and, as far as I can remember, no treatment. The MO flared up because I did not know what was wrong. I told him I had been bleeding and he asked me to get a specimen. I had but one thought: to get out of such an undignified situation. The official label for the MO's judgment on my case was 'medicine and duty'. As the day's working party had left — I felt a little conscience-stricken about this — I was assigned to duties at the field kitchen. Dixie-cleaning seemed even less attractive than road-mending.

On the return of the working party, which Jimmy told me had again been uneventful, we were each issued with two Mills bombs, two Very lights, two sandbags and an extra two hundred rounds of small-arms ammunition, a significant addition to our existing load and an indication of an early move into livelier parts, about which rumour had already become active.

That evening I was feeling better physically, but sore at heart. Sitting on a heap of rubble above the rotting trenches that sheltered the majority of the company I could survey the war-blasted earth, seared and broken by the barrages that had fallen upon the enemy positions in front of Mametz Wood. The ground rose slowly to the smashed trees, still matted together with an almost impenetrable undergrowth of saplings, wire and other debris, where there were trenches hidden and all the unexplored horrors of battle. Many of the dead were still unburied. They were not in the way and their decent disposal seemed to be nobody's business.

Souvenir hunting went on, but such gruesome ferreting was not for me. Apart from picking up some small German fuse caps in neighbouring shell-holes I had, just then, little desire to join the insensitive foragers. Over to the west, in the direction away from the line, where the monotonous desolation eventually reached the areas of the camps, enemy shells were bursting, for they had not our good fortune of being sheltered from observation by the wood itself. Watching the spurting fountains of black earth and flame, I discovered myself calculating the time lapse between the visual burst and the sound of the explosion. It was difficult at that distance to visualize the agony of those who might be involved in each burst. I was thankful not to be there and not a little fearful lest the German gunners might begin searching a little further forward.

It is so easy to assume an attitude of academic neutrality to events however dire that are not within one's own range of experience. That is why gunners and airmen do their jobs with mathematical efficiency, at the end of their long strung-out processes, without suffering undue qualms. That evening as I sat with that frightening panorama around me my feelings of homesickness were barely supportable. Yet I knew full well that this was but the beginning, the mere prelude to something too awful to contemplate.

The next day, the last of the month, took us away again on working party. Our job was to let a large water-pipe into the ground alongside the main road near Bazentin-le-Petit. It was a relief to watch the passing traffic, so varied despite its khaki drabness. We laboured under the instructions of Royal Engineers, whose bother was to get the job finished and not to worry about discipline. As usual I found the labour too monotonously uninteresting to chain my thoughts to the immediate surroundings.

Among the gang there was a good deal of joking and cursing. The main topic of discussion was the end of the war, which everyone eagerly desired but whose advent they doubted before death intervened. I gathered that in the high summer the armies had been full of hope, but now progress was so slow that doubts had become stronger than hope. Strange to relate, however, in view of previous experience, there was a strongly optimistic section who still believed that the next blow would do the trick. They said in support that German prisoners now coming across were not of the type we had been led to expect and that, except for the officers, they always seemed glad to be out of the fighting.

We were pleased to have completed our task shortly after lunch break and to get back to camp soon after 3.00 p.m. But here we were met with bad news, for we were ordered immediately to pack and to stand to. Those whom we had left behind were already prepared and the field kitchen had gone off in advance.

As usual in the army everything was begun in a rush, and then we seemed to hang about interminably. I remember to this day sitting on the edge of our shell-hole alongside my equipment, a massive pile now, and listening to the conversation of some officers seated outside a nearby dug-out. They were not of our unit and therefore not getting ready to move. Young, well-washed, with clean uniforms they talked in educated voices that it did me good to hear. They were discussing their feelings under fire and their conclusions have always remained in my mind. I was at that moment particularly apprehensive about how I should behave under fire and my chief fear was that I should be so terrified as to be cowardly and, worse still, show it. They already knew how they felt and how they reacted. They recognized the inevitability of fear and wanted to probe the chief reason for it. They came to a conclusion, which I think was unanimous and with which I completely failed to agree. They said that they feared not so much death as pain and mutilation: they had vividly pictured in their minds the awful agonies of the seriously wounded who could still feel. They were concerned with feeling in its starkest reality.

But my overwhelming fear was not of agony but of extinction, of just going out, of losing one's life almost before it had begun, of dying amidst all the murk without even a friend to say goodbye. I was afraid not merely of dying, but of dying just there where we were, far outside the bounds of the life we really knew. This is the only philosophical discussion that I remember from those days, and I remember it vividly. I wonder whether those men, probably somewhat older than myself, did die in the agony that they feared or survived through the rest of the war and perhaps still live, their important discussion long forgotten amidst many of equal interest to them? But although I had much still to learn and my worst experiences were ahead of me, I never saw reason to change the viewpoint that I had silently taken up on the fringes of their influence. By virtue of my different upbringing and my different outlook I was the silent opposition whose existence they did not suspect.

Orders came at last for us to move. Each was given a pick or shovel to add to his load and we moved off along the track through the blasted wood, wearily from the outset. I was cold, tired and hungry, and with the weight every step soon became an agony. The pace was set by the lightly clad officers and more robust members of the company who strode forward with exemplary eagerness to get the journey over. The column soon began to stretch out. The road of rounded tree-trunks laid in parallel cross-wise was particularly uncomfortable. In my mind's eye it began to heave and lurch like a sea, and the daylight seemed to lower to an unreal glow, although it was still long before sunset. Only a regulation halt saved me from collapsing, as I slipped to the erratic but welcoming track in a heap.

Already the column was straggling far back into the narrow defile amidst the arboreal garbage where but a few months earlier birds had nested and sung. It was clear that as a body we were not sufficiently trained or physically attuned to make even such a modest effort. Yet nobody seemed to bother. It was this that made it all so much worse. Nobody really cared what happened. An occasional uninterested 'keep up, there' from one of the NCOs was all the notice that authority took. Jimmy confided that he could not keep up and suggested that I should concentrate on ensuring a place for us wherever our destination might be. We were now fully conscious of the fight that went on unendingly between the old hands and the new, a sort of parochial fight for survival within the boundaries of the greater fight for survival. We guessed why the comparatively active and fit ones in front were eager to get forward. I had grave doubts of my capacity to run in this race but resolved to do my best.

Somehow I did manage to keep going nearer to the head of the column which soon became strung out deep into the wood behind. We left the wood, crossed the main road and, skirting another wood on our right, reached a system of trenches similar to the one we had vacated but now situated in front of the wood on the side towards the enemy, with open rolling country, abandoned and deserted, extending to the horizon. The first arrivals advised us to take cover without delay. Our plight proved as bad as before. The few dug-outs in the trench were occupied or commandeered for officers, NCOs, runners, bombers, machine-gunners, in fact, for everybody who claimed privileged status in accordance with the specialist organization that had developed at that stage of the war. I was too inexperienced then to understand, but this was an immature, almost spontaneous, example of a caste society in the making: we, the latecomers, were the pariahs who belonged nowhere. It was 1916 and the war had begun in 1914. It was only right and proper that our suffering should be the greater and our burden the heaviest, the long vistas ahead into 1917 and 1918 were not yet in men's minds, for even to the least optimistic the war seemed likely suddenly to terminate with some miraculous turn of fate that the present slow progress was merely masking. Over the horizon was the enemy, many times defeated, and the countryside beyond, where the trees still lived and the fields remained green.

Even now we were merely on the far edge of the battlefield. The scene had a sterile, deserted look and yet one felt the presence of movement hidden below ground and away in dark corners. It no longer seemed right to be walking above ground, and only those who had no shelter were doing so. In many directions heavy shells were falling, throwing up the black threatening fountains which I was beginning to know, but none very close at hand, though tiredness now blunted the perception of danger.

I was worried about shelter and about Jimmy, who had not yet appeared. Disburdened of my equipment I was soon able to go in search of him. I found him among the stragglers and told him of our predicament. Hot tea from the kitchen having revived us, we set about constructing another bivouac on previous lines in a hole not far from the trench: this was the best we could do. Then the mail came up and we were each heartened by the arrival of parcels from home. There was no greater delight in that world than receiving such a gift, containing all those little extras that made so much difference. The nucleus of every such war parcel was usually a large home-made cake. Every day in all parts of the beloved homeland dear, devoted, feminine hands were assembling these tributes to the absent ones, depositing them in the care of the General Post Office, as in the past offerings had been reverently placed upon shrines, and there was inherent truth in this attitude. Yet despite all that, it is doubtful whether those at home could fully realise the great benediction that such modest gifts invariably brought to the homeless and spiritually alone.

That night too, in further compensation, I had my first rum ration, or only half a ration, for that was all I could stomach of this strange new liquid. It burned my throat and tasted vile, but the ensuing warmth in such circumstances had to be experienced to be believed. I soon became used to the taste and forgot any leanings towards teetotalism when the rum ration came up.

On the following morning we awoke early, refreshed and feeling stronger. By 6.30 a.m., armed with shovel or pick, we left the reserve position, for such it was, and moved out of the wood and past Bazentin-le-Petit, an immense rubbish heap of shattered buildings which had been cordoned off and boldly sign-posted. As we skirted the windward side the horrible stench of unburied dead filled our nostrils. The sickly smell of rotting humanity, which we were to come to know too well so that it almost seeped into our dreams, overhung the pulverized village like a pall above a dreadful communal tomb, as indeed it was.

This was to be my day of initiation. On a busy road leading from the village northwards towards High Wood, we were detailed to fill in pot-holes. Work had not long commenced when a whining noise presaged the approach of a shell. I ducked as it burst some way down the road which was clearly the enemy's target. I felt paralysed with fear. This was it, then. No one else seemed to take any notice. The road ran through a shallow cutting with banks on either side. There seemed to be no escape. We worked on. The shelling continued at intervals. Some fell so near that pieces of red-hot shrapnel spanged into the mud at my feet. Traffic continued to stream by at intervals. A little way along the road an artillery driver was killed in his driving seat, the only casualty in my vicinity.

The enemy decided to alter his range and concentrate on the point where the road topped the low ridge by High Wood. There a working party of the Durham Light Infantry were caught in the storm and came off much worse than we had. We could see the shells bursting among them and men running for shelter. Shortly a horrible procession began to pass back along the road. Several cases, mangled and bloody, were carried by on stretchers, while others with hand or foot swathed in bandages hobbled past, grimly intent upon getting away from the dangerous place. Then all was quiet again and we continued with our rather futile task.

During the lunch rest some of the party explored the neighbouring field which still remained very much as the tide of battle had left it. A yellow-faced Tommy, half-leaning, still transfixed with his bayonet a black-faced Fritz: death had come to them almost simultaneously and no one had yet bothered to consider their condition — unless it was to rifle their pockets. One glimpse of this horrible tableau was enough for me. Others, less squeamish, went foraging for souvenirs among sights that, if their accounts were true, were equally horrifying. I had no stomach for the secrets of that hellish field. Here imagination was hardly needed to embellish the truth. This was one of those days on which I was growing up fast. The very air around us now seemed charged with apprehension, though there were no more untoward incidents. I felt a great relief when the order came to pack up. As I marched back in the silent column my mind was filled with fears that no longer lacked reality for their shaping. The truth I was coming to know was beyond all my imagining.

It was on Sunday, 1st October that I first went into battle. We were awakened at 6.00 a.m. and ordered to get our kits ready for the trenches. Despite our actual presence in reserve during the preceding days, this command still had an element of the unexpected and its real implications took a little time to sink in. We were not told what was afoot but learned about it, as it were, in snatches as events unfolded.

The night had been noisy and damp. Shells had fallen in the fields and woods around, but despite these discomforts I had been too tired to experience more than a half fear. I had slept well enough. We gave in our packs, adjusted our equipments to battle-order and put on our steel helmets. Some still preferred their old shapeless trench caps of the 'Old Bill' style. Loaded with bombs and other personal extras, as well as cans of water, boxes of Mills grenades and other impedimenta, we moved off at 10.00 a.m.

We had first to cross the deserted belt that divided the reserve and heavy-gun areas from the trenches proper. The thin khaki file crawled with a snake-like movement across this desolate land towards the low ridge beyond which the present battle-line lay. Our immediate objective was a communications trench which dented the ridge. As far as I was concerned we could not get there quickly enough, but there was no altering the measured tempo of our advance, though I am sure that those in front were as eager as I to get away from the exposed place. Heavy shells were now falling all over the area, yet none within a hundred yards or so. Earth and muck rose high into the air and fell back like a drooping fountain. I heard spent shrapnel droning into the mud. We must have been about fifty yards from the trench when the man behind drew attention to my water bottle and at the same time I felt a sticky fluid soaking into my trousers. The lemonade, which I had mixed from the powder contained in my parcel, was running out. A round shrapnel bullet had entered the enamel bottle at the flat side with enough force to turn almost at right angles and pierce the enamel a second time, then to lodge under the canvas cover which it had not enough force left to break. It seemed that at this early stage I had narrowly escaped a 'blighty'. I felt aggrieved with fate, but a sergeant who had shown enough interest in the incident to display my damaged bottle to the officer, had a less optimistic diagnosis. The bullet had been travelling straight into my side and had been deflected. Clearly it had arrived with sufficient force to cause a serious, possibly a fatal wound in those regions of the body. At the time I could discern no miracle, but the loss of my drink worried me, for to go waterless into action was a serious matter, even on this muddy battle-field.

Shortly after midday we reached the support lines where the company was to remain while a battalion of the Durham Light Infantry assaulted Le Sars. The surrounding ground was a dirty brown of slime and mud, criss-crossed here and there with trenches, but on the horizon beyond the enemy's positions were trees and open country. Our minds filled in with green fields and leafy lanes, now turning russet with autumn tints, the scene which we could only distantly sense. In our vicinity, here and there a gaunt tree pointed its wounded limbs with ludicrous inconsequence to the skies. The trench, deep and duck-boarded, was well made, but here and there through its revetted sides objects of horrible promise showed themselves — abandoned equipment, a boot or a piece of uniform — and I had no doubt the remains of an unmarked hero were not far away. I gathered as a souvenir a black tunic button stamped with crown and trumpet of a rifle regiment.

The day's objective was the little village of Le Sars on the Albert-Bapaume road. It was towards the key point of Bapaume that the battle had been slowly converging during the past weeks and the enemy was contesting every foot of the way. Rumour now had it that Bapaume was the essential prize with whose capture the great battle that had begun on 1st July would be won. The bones and blood of victory and vanquished were already fertilizing the evil-smelling loam around us.

In a recess just behind us a Vickers machine-gun had been set up to assist in the barrage that would protect the attackers. Otherwise there was little to indicate that a battle was about to surge forth. The enemy was to be taken by surprise. Guns continued to fire desultorily from both sides. Shells burst here and there but none near our trench. The old hands warned us against complacency. We were supports, to be sent for and used wherever needed, and the enemy could be expected to do all he could to prevent our taking a hand. Our static position was among the least enviable in an action of this sort. The logic of this discouraging advice was not lost upon us. We waited.

Suddenly the machine-guns opened out with an ear-splitting rattle, spraying a long-distance stream of bullets over the lines, and the artillery behind quickly joined in, until the bombardment rose to a continuous roar such as I had never heard before. A regular ceiling of shells was rushing overhead to form an advancing curtain of fire ahead of the attacking troops. The enemy's counter-bombardment soon began, but frankly this was something of an anti-climax after what we had heard. Shells were falling all over the place or bursting in the air above, but there was no real concentration on our position. It all seemed part of the intended scheme and I soon began to feel much more confident and warlike. I learned then, as I was to recognize time after time later, that one well-directed shell could cause as much fear and consternation as a whole bombardment. It is fortunate that there is a limit to the total of fear that an ordinary man can experience at any one time.

Very shortly a crackle of machine-gun and rifle fire, insinuating itself through the greater uproar, indicated that battle had been joined on the ground and that the enemy were resisting stoutly. I was not so unmindful of the suffering of others to fail to give a thought to those who were at the moment involved in the hurricane of death, and I was detached enough to regard my own situation as of little moment.

The Durhams were successful: two lines of trenches had been taken. Towards the end of the afternoon the shelling began to die away. But by this time the flow of wounded had begun, some along the trench but many over the top with little attempt to take cover. Eagerness to get away as quickly as possible had overcome any fear of further disaster, though this in fact too often occurred. One party I shall never forget. They were walking cases, some bandaged. All were gesticulating, shaking and capering like men demented, as, for the time being, they were, wounded in the mind rather than in the body. They were the first shell-shocked cases that I had seen, and as they passed across the trench and away out of sight, they composed a horrid frieze of unhappy humanity that remains graven in my mind more than a half century later, the grimmest scene on the day I first experienced a real battle.

Towards dusk the company was ordered forward into the communication trenches to support the front line in case of enemy counter-attack. Groping our way slowly along tortuous alleys, obstructed at every turn by loose telephone wires difficult to see in the dark, we packed up as far forward as possible. Runners and other details continually jostled by as they proceeded upon their business. At places the trench narrowed so much as to render such passage almost impossible. Artillery officers, Royal Engineers, ration parties, wounded Durhams and German prisoners all struggled by, eager to get somewhere else. The prisoners were in the main a docile-looking crowd, much to my astonishment at that time. Here were not the fire-eating Boche of the daily press but ordinary men who could not avoid showing their undoubted relief at the prospect of getting away from it all. They were roundly cursed — as were most of the passers by — but rarely molested, though I did see one of the company kick a passing prisoner viciously. The Northumberlands were certainly a wild crowd with normally little sympathy for the defeated, but this nevertheless was an unusual incident in my personal experience. We knew too well in our hearts that those others had no greater liking for the ordeal than we had.

Enemy lights constantly illuminated the skies ahead, throwing into relief, over the ridge of earth that marked the edge of the trench, a row of broken tree trunks and a forest of barbed wire pickets that seemed to accentuate the desolation. The firing was general from both sides and shells seemed to be brushing over in every direction. Near the trench a battery of field guns was hammering away and at first I found it difficult to distinguish enemy shell-bursts from the resonant reports issuing from the gun-pits. The air was so filled with droning shrapnel that I was surprised no one was hit. In view of our packed-up condition it would have paid the enemy to concentrate his fire upon the communication trenches.

The long night wore on in a sort of nightmarish slow-motion. Occasionally we were moved forwards or backwards or round corners, undecidedly. We were in the way and a nuisance to everyone who had legitimate business along the trench. At one point I remember the Captain asking for a volunteer to convey a message across the open to another section. His voice seemed to come from far away, as through a mist, and I tried to delude myself that I was not among those addressed. A successful journey, he suggested, might well bring a recommendation. To have got out of that trench alone with that racket going on would have left me paralyzed with fear and quite incapable of doing anything that depended upon my own initiative. One of the old hands volunteered.

Despite the turmoil, sleepiness began to master my fear and I nodded as I crouched at the bottom of the trench.

Consciousness returned intermittently as a passing foot scraped over my back or a dangling entrenching tool gave me a sharp rap on the head. Towards dawn the noise of battle at last subsided and it became clear that the expected counter-attack was not going to materialize. We were ordered back to our old position.

With feelings of relief our tongues were loosened. The old hands were unanimous that this affair had not been as bad as the attacks they had previously experienced. It was reported, however, that the Durhams had suffered heavy casualties, and we could count ourselves fortunate. I was to learn that these things were very chancy. I took a piece of cheese and some scraps of hard biscuit from my ration bag, now nearly empty, and felt somewhat revived. Sleep would have been welcome, but it was out of the question. My main concern throughout the affair had been my damaged waterbottle, a mishap which my mind seemed to magnify out of all proportion. I had lost no opportunity to ask all and sundry whether they had seen a spare lying about. Eventually I did lay my hands on a bottle whose owner would never again use.

It was a cold morning. Fortunately there was room in our part of the trench to walk up and down to maintain circulation. Later on an officer came along to select a party to fetch bombs from the dump. We clambered out of the trench but a wave of shelling drove us back helter-skelter. The enemy was alert to the least movement. Our leader decided to proceed along the trench. Somewhere ahead one of the shells had burst right in the trench, killing one man and severely wounding another. To cross the damaged sector we had to climb over the debris.

The dead man lay amidst earth and broken timber. It seemed like sacrilege to have to step over him, but there was no evading the issue. Never before had I seen a man who had just been killed. A glance was enough. His face and body were terribly gashed, as though some terrific force had pressed him down, and blood flowed from a dozen fearful wounds. The smell of blood mixed with the fumes of the shell filled me with nausea: only a great effort saved my limbs from giving way under me. I caught up with the file in front, half ashamed of my feelings. But I could see from the sickly grey of their faces that these were generally shared. A voice seemed to whisper, with unchallengeable logic, 'Why shouldn't you be the next?' I could think of no special virtue that should excuse me the fate of so many others.

The trench abruptly turned a corner: the bomb store appeared in a low pit away from the trench in the middle distance, approachable only over the top. It was camouflaged from observation by a covering of sacking, crusted with the mud of the surrounding field. Wicked-looking spurts of black fume were shooting up all over the area, which was at the very centre of the bombardment. It seemed to me a sensible thing to wait, but authority had already decided that the operation must go ahead without delay. We were to run at intervals to the pit, a distance of about fifty yards, withdraw a box of grenades and bring it back.

As if by a miracle the shelling stopped. I awaited my turn tremblingly. Then I climbed out of the trench, ran for dear life, and was on the way back with my load almost before I could realize. The wide open sky all around seemed to be bursting with the threat of sudden death. As I ran breathlessly I expected to hear the approaching screech that had so recently come within my experience. If fear could have killed, then I would have died of fright. But I did not die, and as I leaned panting and thankful against the welcoming earth of the trench I knew the counter-joy of escape that arises only on the battlefield, when the expectation of death comes more often to those who live than to those who die. The last man had just slipped back into the trench when the shelling recommenced. The officer's decision not to dilly-dally, as I should have done, had been fully justified.

It rained all the afternoon. We had no shelter; water began to collect on the trench bottom; everything became slimy and beastly. Then came the bombshell: we were to relieve the Durhams in the line. Poor devils, they needed it badly enough, but this thought hardly reconciled us to the task ahead. We groused and cursed vehemently, failing at that moment to remember that hitherto we had got off very lightly.

Our guide arrived at 6.00 p.m., and we were ready to start. The rain continued. By chance I found myself near the head of the file in a position to hear the conversation of our leaders. The Captain told the senior NCO that the journey was likely to be difficult. This was putting it mildly. The trenches were slippery: we were loaded with boxes of grenades or cans of water. Every now and again the leaders stopped to confer and argue about the correct route. We were in a maze. Not that there was anything exceptional in the situation. My recollection is that officers were rarely sure of their route even when an experienced guide was at hand. Our halts provided us with welcome rests, but they proved also opportunities to freeze, and we were glad to be moving again until fatigue got the upper hand once more, usually after only a few paces.

The route twisted and turned, we hurried and we dallied, now above ground and now below. In the open the fear of shrapnel masked our tiredness, in the trenches we stumbled over one another's heels and called down the direst punishments upon those whom we hated least. The mud was now everywhere, at times an inch or so of sticky gripping soil, at others a mess of liquid filth in which we waded to the knees. Girders spanned the trench forcing us to stoop low, loose wires at our feet lay ready to trip us, higher wires cut across our necks.

And so, hour after hour, the company blundered forward. Every step became heavier as time passed, or seemed to pass, for the whole night had gone into slow motion. At one stage, when our route ran parallel behind the front trench, I had a hazy notion of red lights bobbing up and down amid heavy shell-fire and general turmoil. A counter-attack was being fought off close at hand, but a kind of semi-consciousness had descended upon me to minimize all fear. Fortunately the rain had now stopped. I had hardly the strength to drag one foot ahead of the other, and my companions were in no better shape. We had no alternative but to go on. My box of Mills grenades had proved too heavy and slipped to the ground at some dark corner. This, I fear, was the fate of most of the extra supplies, which we might so urgently need later. But what could one do about it?

The shelling again became more intense. We were certainly crossing a battlefield, but it was no concern of ours. We had to relieve the Durhams wherever they might be. Under stress and fatigue, fear had diminished almost to zero. I had reached the state, which I was to experience again, when one's active mind speculates objectively about one's fate. What were the chances of Private Gladden getting a nice little blighty? Or would he perhaps prefer to die as a release from present agony which seemed likely to go on endlessly?

Suddenly, it seemed, we had arrived. A few steps led down to a sunken road. Shouts to hurry: it was dangerous here. Shadowy forms waiting motionless in the gloom; a right-hand turn into a trench; stooping figures under huge packs riding them like jockeys; grunts of satisfaction. The relief was in at last and the battle-weary Durhams filed silently away into the night. It was 3.30 a.m. Incredibly our comparatively short journey had taken nine and a half hours. I sank exhausted to the mud.

'Come on, stand to,' bawled a voice in my ear. Dawn was approaching. It was freezing. How long I had been unconscious I do not know. This was an unforgivable crime. The enemy could have taken us all by surprise, had he suspected. But apparently nobody was troubled. Now the NCOs began to bustle about and demonstrate their zeal. We took up positions along the edge of the trench, if trench it could be called, for hereabouts it was many yards wide, sloping up to each rim like a large bowl and affording little cover. We fixed bayonets and stood ready with Mills bombs. Our rifles were clogged with mud and could not have been of much use. I prayed devoutly that nothing would happen for I was sure I should be helpless in an emergency. The guns began a stand-to strafe on both sides. Our shells seemed to be just skimming the parapet, frightening us as much as the enemy. I expected one to burst upon us at any moment. Nor was this, as I learned later, an uncommon occurrence.

The day dawned slowly as we shivered along the edge of the trench. We seemed in the new light to be marooned in a sea of mud and slime. To our right the trench narrowed and deepened, ending abruptly against a barrier of earth. We were in a cul-de-sac. Against the dead-end a bombing section had been stationed, on guard against an enemy group who had re-occupied the rest of the trench after Sunday's advance. To our left the trench narrowed to normal proportions and there, on the wrong side, facing the enemy-line, gaped the openings of a number of abandoned dug-outs. Despite the presence of the enemy on our right we were actually in a switch line behind the main forward positions which had been taken over by other companies of our battalion.

The ground vibrated under shell bursts, as though a big drum were being beaten, and fantastic new fears gripped my receptive mind. The prospect of being blown up by a mine, vivified by some description I had read, had always seemed to me the most terrifying prospect of death, although I must admit that this was not a very frequent occurrence even in trench warfare and only then when the situation was static.

A shout of alarm suddenly redirected my thoughts. We began to pull at the safety pins of our Mills bombs: something was about to happen. And then, as if from nowhere, the figure of a German soldier appeared over the parapet. He was a fine-looking fellow, tall and military, dressed in the garb I had so often seen depicted in magazines — *Pickelhaube* on his head, high boots, even wearing a finely waxed Kaiser-moustache. Nothing more unexpected or unlikely, for that matter, could have fallen within our vision. At any other time we should have laughed. The stranger advanced with his arms above his head and was hustled away towards the Captain's dug-out.

Everyone now was on the alert; naturally we feared some sort of trap, but soon word was passed along that the German — actually a sergeant-major of infantry — had come to arrange the surrender of his companions behind the barrier who had become isolated from their own unit. Two others would come over in advance and if they were received without hurt the rest would follow at intervals. We were ordered not to molest them unless serious suspicions were aroused. And so it all came to pass. During the morning about seventy in all gave themselves up. They were very different from the pictorialized version of the German soldier which the first arrival had endorsed. Smaller of stature, shabby and worn-looking, they seemed without exception to be meek men who were gratified and perhaps a little surprised at being received with a certain rough kindness.

The appearance of these men on the battlefield, the first of the enemy I had seen off-stage, as it were, caused me a mild shock. Clearly these were not the same men who had rushed enthusiastically to arms two years before and perpetrated those horrors upon the civilians of Belgium and Northern France, as part of Germany's quick victory policy. I continued to muse over the strangeness of this war, even to wondering with some amusement why each side did not give itself up to the other. That would confound the strategists on both sides. No doubt our haul of prisoners would redound to the credit of the battalion which had in fact made no special effort to bring it about.

The day wore on and I was surprised how easily I had become accustomed to living with danger. During the afternoon an adjoining brigade delivered a local attack to straighten out the line. We stood to, expecting a counter-blast from the enemy. Our guns opened out and shortly word came back that the objective had been gained with little difficulty. The enemy remained quiet on our sector until the evening, when he began a methodical strafe of the position. As it had but recently been his trench he knew every inch of the ground.

Now for the first time I was to know what it was really like to be in the target area. We moved into the narrower parts of the trench which would provide the best protection and the old hands, having assured themselves of good cover, advised us to spread out. This sound military precept, we did not follow. We bunched and cowered to the earth which we had never loved so much. I felt that death was now inevitable. As each screeching shell approached, it seemed directed not merely towards me but at my head which I sought to protect at all costs. I was consumed by a dreadful demoralizing fear. Each burst rocked the earth, filled the air with mud and shrapnel and the smell of cordite. After each blast I was filled with an amazed gratitude at still being whole.

I was crouching near one of those yawning dug-outs facing the front, a regular death trap should a shell burst near the top. Yet one by one, men in desperation were pushing into the opening. I saw Jimmy's white terror-ridden face disappearing from sight and, unable to stand more, I followed him, cowering in the shelter of the overhanging earth. The dug-out steps dipped away into the blackness and shouts of protest came from the depths as each new entrant compelled those below to move further down. A hideous stench of Germans already disintegrating below struck me, as by a blow, causing me to recoil in revulsion. It was too much. Physical danger was preferable to that horror. I rushed hopelessly back into the trench to escape being trapped.

There was no human movement now. Men crouched in corners, others crammed the dug-out entrances, one or two stood by the parapet keeping watch on the enemy positions. Always in such situations there are the few who continue doing their duty at whatever cost to themselves. As yet I had not acquired such stoicism. Another near explosion forced me back into the opening where I decided to bear the stench for the misleading advantage of the sheltering earth.

At last the bombardment ceased as inconsequentially as it had begun and the calm of evening settled over the brown damp landscape. Unexpectedly, but to our infinite joy, we were told that the relief was on the way. At half past ten the trek out began. The road was rough but we kept above ground and the going was much easier than when we came in. Yet the amelioration was only relative. I was weak, hungry, thirsty and inexpressibly tired. Hour after hour we seemed to move through the darkness with only hope to spur us on. It must have been past 3.00 a.m. when we staggered into the old camp behind Mametz Wood, our last energies oozing away. A drink of hot tea from the steaming field kitchen put a heavenly warmth into my body. The kind of damp ground made a couch of welcome for my weary limbs. No chill morning air could hold back that sleep of exhaustion.

Thus I had endured my first battle and there was little in it that matched my expectations. I had wandered in an unreal world, a damp, muddy, stinking world more horrible than anything I had visualized. The stench of death lingered in my nostrils for days after, almost tangible in its reality. I had seen death in all its horror; experienced the most devastating fear; even worse, I had observed gesticulating men who had lost control of their reason. Yet nothing much had happened. For so it seemed to me at the time. There was a sense of anti-climax. To suffer so much for so little seemed the final indignity. I had yet to realize that humanity is too dwarfed by the vagaries of death and the mere vastness of the mechanics of modern war to be other than a puppet amidst the incomprehensible. The company's function during those few days had been something like that of a pawn in a game of chess.

V: THE BATTALION RESTS

I awoke the next morning on that hard, exposed couch considerably refreshed. On the damp ground and in the cold October air, without any other protection than that afforded by a top coat, one would have thought that sleep would have been impossible, but I was quickly becoming inured to sleeping in impossible conditions and fully prepared to ignore the possibility that neither war nor the elements might awaken one from a sleep of exhaustion before it was too late. What amazes me now is how my generation, who were not brought up to hardships of this sort, managed to survive such experiences. It is true that some did not, but I, who was not particularly robust at that time and might have been considered a certain victim, did survive and apparently with no hurt. On that grim autumn morning I still had much to endure, and it is a mercy that the future is hidden from us, for in the face of the truth few of us would have had even the desire to survive. Today of course the perspectives are very different and now we would not for all the world have missed the experience which, had the chance arisen, we would then have done so much to avoid.

For the first time I experienced the elation that comes from the realization that one has escaped death. I had been in battle and was henceforth a different being, perhaps for the first time I felt myself a man, indefinably changed through having undergone this particular ordeal. True, it had been a very different experience from what I had imagined. There had been nothing heroic about it, and as far as one could see, it would have made little difference had we not been there. Even the pervading sense of danger was negative in retrospect. Yet that morning the drab, dejected surroundings of the shattered wood seemed bright with promise. Indeed our hearts leaped when we were told that the battalion was going out of the line for a spell. A new friendliness was manifested in a company that hitherto had appeared to be at war within itself. We were going back, away from all that.

Our packs were reissued to us before we took the road. There was no question in those days of things being made too easy for the infantry who had to get about everywhere under their own power, carrying all their belongings. The roads were swimming with liquid mud, the effect of which was not apparent at the outset but soon began to tell. We found the going extremely difficult and my previous fatigue quickly returned. But we were going in the right direction and there was every reason to stumble onwards hopefully. Halts were frequent, for our leaders too were weary and the usual regulations could be relaxed to some extent.

For the first time I heard the company singing — a little pathetically perhaps — and for the first time I heard of the amorous adventures of a certain Mademoiselle from Armentieres who 'jiggy-jigged' for souvenirs. That night we slept in a tenantless house that had lost all its upper storeys, in the shadow of the shattered cathedral of Albert, and the following day found us in new billets in the little rural community of Millencourt, five kilometres back from the city.

Millencourt, a undistinguished little village, was situated in the area immediately behind the original line, outside the battle zone. Most of its inhabitants were still there, although some buildings had been evacuated. The fields were remarkably green and unscarred by war, the trees were whole, with swaying branches and leaves assuming their autumn colours. For the first time I was really aware of the countryside as something different, alive and peaceful and sympathetic. Our billet was a farm building on the main thoroughfare, its walls crumbling despite their enlacement by strong wooden beams whose main purpose for us was for hanging up our clothes and equipment.

The floor was of beaten earth with uneven surface, which not only soon became very dirty but provided a very uncomfortable base for our groundsheets and the few blankets at our disposal. The billet smelt of damp earth and departed cattle. It was constant dusk within, a dusk lit by candles which were our only means of illumination. In that war the candle had again become a necessity of life, both in the line and in billet. As few of the official issue reached the ordinary soldier, the local shops did a thriving trade in their crude tallow variety which rapidly burned away. Consequently candles, of our more efficient British variety, became a very popular item in parcels from home.

Inside the billet, especially towards bed-time, the barn looked like a shrine with the numerous illuminants perched upon every ledge and stuck into every suspended mess-tin lid or other receptacle and throwing mysterious shadows among the roof beams. We were to find sleep difficult for, apart from the uneven floor, the barn, not having been built for human habitation, was extremely draughty. Every current of air seemed to concentrate upon our feet which insisted upon protruding out of the blankets into the stark coldness of the night.

The village shop was kept by homely French folk, whose prices were understandably proportionate to the high demands upon their supplies. The latter included, apart from the candles already mentioned, *petit beurre* biscuits in packets, insubstantial cakes, chocolate in bars, various odds and ends for cleaning, and a somewhat sickly syrup called grenadine. Mixed up with our eternal bully-beef stew, these incongruous additions were sufficient to make many of our company feel decidedly ill by our very first evening.

That first day, which happened to be a bright one, was devoted to relaxation and exploration, but I was unfortunate to be detailed for mess-orderly duties, a job at which we took turns and which I never liked. It entailed menial tasks at the cook-house, serving the meals and clearing up afterwards. Except on a day off, such as this one, the job did have its compensations. Orderlies could be sure of a square meal, and they were excused ordinary parades and other duties. Like the housewife they were always on but usually could find periods during the day when they could take things easy. At 9.15 p.m. roll was called by the platoon Sergeant, in our case a bright young man with lance-corporal stripes awaiting promotion, who had the faculty of keeping out of the way unless there were officers about.

On the following day, after an uncomfortable night, my military education was further extended. It did seem somewhat officious to get us out at 7.00 a.m., just when one felt that sleep might really be wooed, and run us round the village in our shirt-sleeves for a constitutional. After that most of the morning was spent in preparing for inspection by the Captain, while in the afternoon our kits had to be laid out in regulation order for a detailed examination. Pay parade at 5.00 p.m. sounded a brighter note and I was both pleased and surprised to receive twenty francs, at that time quite a useful amount. On those occasions we single men received more than the married whose total pay was usually reduced by additional allowances which they allocated to their wives, who got little enough in any case. I was particularly fortunate in this respect as my mother received my Civil Service salary after deduction of the normal army pay. Even now the standard pay was little more than a shilling a day, only the technical experts such as members of the Army Service Corps and the Royal Engineers, and our Dominion forces receiving a daily rate that made them well off in comparison.

By the third day I had lost all my illusions. After the early morning constitutional we found ourselves subjected to a complete time-table of parades and exercises. That day's programme was typical of so many others like it. The morning period from 9.00 a.m. to noon was spent on rifle inspection and platoon drill. At 2.00 p.m. we went on to musketry practice, finishing up with a strenuous bout of bayonet fighting from 3.00 to 3.30 p.m. On paper and in retrospect this does not seem onerous, but much depended upon the seriousness of the instructors and in any case it was boring for we had done it all so often before. There was nothing in these mechanical movements to keep one's brain occupied. One's thoughts wandered far and wide until something went wrong and one was brought back to reality with a flow of sarcasm and expletives. All this was of course in the peacetime tradition, but there were so many items of trench craft on which we were ignorant that we could have spent the time so much more usefully.

The truth was that we were killing time and we knew it. Tradition dies hard, and as yet we were only two years from those pre-war parade routines that had represented the last word in soldiering. The new army was still permeated with the spirit of the old, admirable in some respects, but terribly antiquated in others. New initiatives were now needed, but so many of our leaders found it so much easier to keep to the book, those little red volumes of King's Regulations which the sergeants treasured as their bibles.

At the end of that first morning of parades the Colonel inspected us. An old regular, he failed to stifle the inherent aversion he had to commanding such a nondescript mob, an understandable feeling in a professional such as he but not one to endear him to us. Two Military Medals, awarded to the battalion, were handed to their recipients while we all stood at attention. One went to the Medical Officer's orderly who had no doubt richly earned it. One's immediate admiration went to the stretcher bearers and medical orderlies who served the stricken under fire. They needed nerves of steel and took more risks than most.

Then the Colonel addressed us, looking down from his horse, his head way up in the clouds. Our recent tour, he said, had been a light one for the battalion which, he was proud to add, had done its job well. A more serious task was to be expected next time. His interest brightened here. We must put our backs into it, and do even better for the glory of the regiment, and so on.... At the mention of the future our hearts sank. The old hands did not hesitate to mutter choice, half-audible imprecations which, it seemed to me, the Colonel could hardly fail to hear. For a brief shivering instant the healthy trees that edged the parade-ground assumed stunted mocking shapes.

That evening, Jimmy and I, following a rumour of a sort of Aladdin's cave, found our way along quiet rural roads to the neighbouring village of Henencourt where the YMCA had set up a large marquee in which was displayed a remarkable assortment of eatables from home. We laid in a store and promised ourselves another visit in a day or so. But that was not to be for the canteen was shortly placed out of bounds. Why this was done, I cannot say, but we had explanations that were far from complimentary to our betters. No one in authority seemed to bother about the effect of such actions, so that all but the most loyal among us came to hold the view that to pull less than one's weight — 'swinging the lead' or 'dodging the column' as it was called — was nothing but commendable.

The next day was Sunday and treated as a real day of rest, except for those unfortunates allocated to orderly duties. I was glad I had so recently had my turn. In the morning we were taken to the army baths, not before time it must be added. Our washing facilities in the billet were quite inadequate, involving the communal use of animal troughs or empty biscuit tins filled with well water which soon became a thick soup. After dinner the Church of England members — the majority — attended church service in one of the barns, while the Roman Catholics, of whom Jimmy was one, and the chapel-goers of various denominations disappeared mysteriously to their own meeting places.

I was glad to be able to spend much of the rest of the time reading and writing letters in the billet. It was already clear to me that our postal communications were not efficient. I was only receiving a trickle of the many papers and magazines that were being despatched from home. There was a leakage somewhere and it is significant that it was only with this particular unit that I suffered this disappointment. Generally speaking the postal services for the troops were highly satisfactory; a matter of great importance, for soldiers on active service live in spirit with those they have left behind and about whose welfare they become exaggeratedly apprehensive. In my experience everyone at home fully understood the position and most of us had among our regular correspondents many for whom, in normal circumstances, the writing of letters would have been a considerable burden.

During our period in billets we came to know our companions better, not that there was any real *rapprochement*. Later I came to understand the Tynesider and to like him a lot, even to speak with his very special brogue, but at that time there was a wall between us. Taken as a whole we were indeed a nondescript group. The old hands seemed to have known one another in civil life, mainly in the pits of Durham and Northumberland. They addressed one another affectionately, frequently using the endearing term 'kidder' and reminiscing about mutual friends at home. The open morals of the village belle were intimately discussed. There were constant sad references to that other, ever-growing band of absentees who had come over with the unit from England and would never return. The barn became peopled with ghosts whom we should never know. They were a clannish crowd and this may have explained our off-hand reception at Mametz Wood. They treated all 'Southerners' with contempt, but to the Cockneys they were not actively hostile. We soon learned that provided we remained neutral we should be left alone and allowed to fit in.

Our Northerners' active hatred was reserved for another type of southerner, the Yorkshiremen, of whom we had an appreciable minority and with whom we found much more in common, although to us they were northerners indeed, far enough from London for the differing degrees of northernness between them and the Geordies to be not worth considering. The antagonism between the two groups was mutual and unrestrained. I could never understand it, and when the two factions were reviling one another I drew back warily anticipating the fight which did sometimes materialize.

It was at mealtimes that the platoon showed up worst. The arrangements were shocking. There was no order or semblance of a queue. As soon as the mess-orderly arrived with the dixie of stew or lid of bacon there was a mad rush in which the receptacle was always in danger of overturn. It was every man for himself and if anyone went without he got no sympathy. The blame was on 'them', the authorities, for not providing enough. Often the Orderly Corporal, who made the company rounds, stood by helplessly. Again this was not to be my normal army experience.

I soon discovered that it was necessary to be on the spot before the melee began and that a measure of foresight and cunning could be more effective than brute force. I was no boxer or physically a match for most of my companions, but I learned at an early stage that it was fatal to give way to intimidation. Under the threat of aggression it was sound tactics to stand firm and look aggressive, even when quaking in one's boots. The bully rarely attempted to press his advantage home.

During the next few days the drills continued, ranging from saluting parades to the inspection of entrenching tools; but there was an even more annoying development in the form of a spit-and-polish campaign. The leather and brass of our equipment had got into a shocking state as a result of too many soakings in mud and slime. It was understandable that the Colonel was not satisfied with our appearance. He would not recognize that there were limits to the degree of polish achievable with the cleaning resources at our disposal. On leaving our home camp we had been told to dump our cleaning tackle as an unnecessary burden on active service. Now there was much borrowing of the few available brushes, hectic scrounging in village shops for boot-polish and requests in letters home for tins of Bluebell and Soldiers' Friend to be enclosed in the next parcel. Clean shirts would have been more to the point, but these would not show up much at inspections.

To cap my current discomforts, on 13th October I captured my first body louse. This shocking event was duly noted in my diary. The lice came out of the blankets which, although periodically treated, literally swarmed with them. I was not again to be free of this disgusting pest as long as I served abroad.

On the following afternoon, after spending the morning at the ranges firing our rifles in gas helmets (a difficult operation in that early type of flannel mask which insisted upon skewing round) and in drawing a new undershirt and cap comforter from the quartermaster's stores, we were switched away from our sylvan surroundings to go out on working parties from Albert. This sudden move, coming out of the blue as such changes usually did, was not much to our liking. As usual authority was heaped with curses; the likelihood that this was the first step back to hell did not sweeten our tempers. Our new billet was again in the shadow of the hanging Madonna, a deserted building which had clearly had ecclesiastical uses, for in a central cloister there stood a statue of Our Saviour. The courtyard, littered with broken masonry and other debris, was not sufficiently shattered to mask all its original peace and beauty. The building, not badly damaged, provided a much more comfortable billet than the barn we had just left.

On the following day we were up on the main road about an hour's march from Albert. Our job was to level an embankment bordering the route at a busy crossing. There were many similar parties at work in the vicinity, so that clearly the job was considered to be one of some importance. We scraped and dug in the chalk all day but the object of our endeavours never became clear to me. Here was the usual breakdown in public relations. We did not expect anything different. As far as the job was concerned it was both tiring and boring to me, as all manual work tended to be. We had a general notion that we were killing time and some, the cunning ones, or lead-swingers, invented their own counter-pastime which often consumed even more energy in avoiding the work than would have been needed to do it.

From the top of the embankment there was an extensive view in all directions. A sea of mud swept around us and away to the curved horizon, splotched here and there with tents and bivouacs, huts and materials heaped in dumps, while over it all, giving it the appearance of some vast ant heap, moved a crawling mass of humanity, which seemed, from that low eminence, as erratic and pointless as the activities of the same industrious well organized insects when moving on the ground beneath ones legs. From the surrounding expanses heavy guns fired spasmodically, their rushing missiles screaming away to that part of the horizon beyond which lay the German positions. Nothing untoward happened.

We arrived back in billet at 5.30 p.m. just eleven hours after we had set out. I had hardly divested myself of my haversack when a sergeant rushed in and ordered me to prepare immediately for guard duties. 'Why me,' my heart piteously questioned, 'so soon after a working party?' 'Why not you?' answered cold reason. 'Someone had to take the duty.' Fortunately this was not to be a ceremonial guard and my instant vision of hectic cleaning and polishing immediately dispersed when I learned that a real job of work was involved — to watch over a condemned water tap. The preliminary inspection was of small moment and our corporal in charge, who had been as annoyed as the rest at being chosen, consoled us with the knowledge that we should miss the next day's working party. He was himself a Northumbrian who had only recently come to the battalion and who put us in good humour by joining heartily in condemning the arbitrary ways of our unit which, he assured us, were unique in his experience.

We spent a quiet, contented day watching that condemned tap and talking over the heart-felt things of a world that seemed so far away. Our Corporal had been there more recently than we, having been invalided home with wounds, and he could give us up-to-date information on home affairs. During the afternoon, with the agreement of the NCO, I went as an emissary of the guard in search of food and small necessaries. As I sallied forth into the deserted streets of Albert it seemed strange to be alone, for there is little privacy in the army. At first I felt happy at the brief respite, the unusual feeling of freedom. The houses around were in the main intact, their gaping windows being the chief sign of their abandonment. Yet over all was an air of melancholy. Here and there homes were still occupied, and it was in such buildings that one found shops with their small stocks of chocolate and other saleable things.

Now and then one came to a gaping void from which an entire house had been extracted like a tooth or smashed in to disclose a set of precariously hanging fireplaces. Sometimes debris still strewed the pavements, indicating a recent explosion and reminding me of the proximity of danger and tragedy.

I found a little shop just off the main square, made all my purchases and started on my homeward journey. At that moment a shell screamed down into a neighbouring street: a brisk bombardment of the district commenced. There was no one else about and I felt less pleased at being alone. I had no compunction in taking to my heels. Flying bricks and spent shrapnel clattered into the roadway and everywhere seemed to be stirred into pandemonium. I was not sorry when I stumbled panting into our post which, as it happened, was just outside the bombarded area.

Shortly the shelling desisted and we settled down to enjoy the fruits of my expedition. A passing runner told us that one of the shells had fallen in the main square near a group of chatting staff officers, killing one and wounding the rest. They must have thought themselves safe enough so far behind the line, but the indiscriminateness of war is a never-ending surprise even to those who have become inured to its vagaries. The last thing that the next-of-kin of that important red-hatted officer could have visualized would have been the off-hand way of his dying in the main square of that deserted town.

I took part in one more of the working parties under the Royal Engineers, who were so difficult to please and literally exuded the impression that they alone were winning the war. We were setting up posts round a site which was in some way to be used for the construction of winter quarters. Then I attended for two days a miniature school which had been established in one of the empty houses to teach the duties of observer and guide, for which work I had been chosen. This seemed to be an excellent stroke of fortune, for it was a good thing to be a specialist in the company. The job of observer was particularly interesting and not without a certain prestige. An officer had been deputed to teach us map-reading and the use of the compass, neither of which were new to me. It may seem ridiculous at this distant date still to recollect one lesson he tried hard to teach us. Annoyed by the frequency with which members of class asked to be excused, he lectured us on the importance of learning to control our natural impulses, a discipline which he considered many of us had lacked from childhood. I remember his lesson but doubt his diagnosis.

Somehow or other nothing came of this brave training impulse. After two days the school closed down and we returned to Millencourt, where we were rejoined by the working party which had stayed up the line for an extra day or two.

The weather was taking a turn for the worse: for some days it had become colder and rain had threatened, now there was a continuous downpour.

On the following day we had leisure between parades to clean and straighten ourselves up again. A new draft joined us, considerably strengthening the Yorkshire element. During the morning a German plane came over, heavily shelled by our guns which trailed it across the sky. At the time enemy planes were fairly active over the lines, observing the forward zones where they seemed usually to fly unmolested, but we did not often see them over the rear areas. As usual this marauder seemed to be getting away but when well on the way towards his own territory we were glad to see him literally drop out of the sky like a stone. That same night his mission was explained by an enemy bombing attack upon the rear areas. No bombs fell on our village but we heard the machine pass over. Then in the early hours the artillery began to rumble all along the front and continued unceasingly throughout the morning.

We knew that another full-scale attack was in progress and our anguished thoughts, vividly heightened by the realities we knew, went out to the poor devils who were taking part.

Two days later we packed up and marched back to Albert, where we were billeted for the night. Our brief 'holiday' was definitely over.

VI: AUTUMN BATTLES — MUD AND THE BUTTE DE WARLENCOURT

On 24th October we left Albert in full marching order for the battle area and the land of mud. It rained. At midday we pulled off the road just short of Bazentin-le-Petit for an issue of stew and tea from the field kitchen which was hard put to produce a meal in the drizzle. We stood about wrapped in our groundsheets and taking advantage of what little shelter there was, a thoroughly miserable band. The traffic streamed by unceasingly, except when the mud claimed a part of it for its own. A limber got badly stuck close by and only after repeated thrashings of the poor mules, aided by hand assistance on the wheels, were the exasperated charioteers able to move on again. Rations, munitions, guns, stores, ambulances, limbers, mules, men; all units, all ranks flowing this way and that, perpetual motion in a sea of filthy, soaking, slimy mud: such was the scene around us, a drab purposeful, inhuman picture as it came to our barely comprehending eyes through the dripping screen that laid its clammy presence about us, adding to the utter desolation in our souls. Never surely were reluctant heroes so unheroically conditioned.

Our resting place was eventually discovered on a rise behind High Wood, in bivouacs, low tent-like shelters, not proof against such weather as that day had brought. The usual rush for shelter took place as soon as the company was dismissed. I looked into two or three shelters which were by no means overcrowded but was made to understand in no unmeasured terms that all the places were reserved. At last in desperation, for it was still raining, I pushed into one close at hand.

Williams, a burly miner whose uncouth, bullying manner I had already noted, occupied the end place. His raised fist moved to within a few inches of my nose as he told me to clear out. I saw a muscular forearm of steel, forged in the Herculean task of cutting coal, and knew that a single blow would settle me. Only the alternative outside compelled me to persist. I had little choice between two evils, except that my spirit was fortified by a strong sense of the injustice of the threat before me. The clenched fist came even closer and then fell away. I crawled under the cover while the threatening figure withdrew towards the middle of the bivouac where there was still plenty of room. Jimmy was now standing helplessly outside. I beckoned him over to follow my example. Another threatening growl came from inside the shelter, but we had found cover and now set about consolidating our position. It is difficult today to visualize the unspectacular desolation of that surrounding expanse of mud, like a sea lapping the bivouacs and indeed oozing within every time one of the occupants moved in or out. The scene was fringed in the middle distance by the gaunt broken tree-shafts of the wood showing fitfully through the drizzle. It is less difficult perhaps to imagine the utter desolation in our souls as we huddled under the clammy canvas. One might now be tempted to wonder why death should seem so awful in such a world.

The following morning the rain had ceased, but everywhere was a quagmire and we spent the day slopping about, fetching and carrying, itching and shivering and feeling thoroughly miserable. During the morning I was pressed into a party detailed to carry bombs from a dump over by High Wood. A closer inspection did nothing to diminish the depressing horror of this spot. The ground around was seared and torn and heaped with all kinds of rubbish. An abandoned tank amidst tree stumps — the first I had seen — struck a comical note. It looked like some mechanical insect designed by Jules Verne or H.G. Wells — two authors to whose books as a schoolboy I had been much addicted — trailing ill a sort of absent-minded way a spare pair of wheels behind it. We certainly had great hopes for this new contraption and were heartened by the feeling that with it our side were one up on the enemy with his undoubted capacity for war-making. A little way from the edge of the wood there also stood a derelict German battery looking as innocuous as toy guns in a table-top battle. The guns were of a light type and calibre shaped very much like toy cannon with their muzzles collared by metal shields from which jagged lumps had been gashed by our shells. In the drab landscape one unusual feature met our eyes, unusual that is to say for that battlefield. On rising ground behind the wood stood the stark walls of a high building whose shape survived despite the fact that its interior had been completely gutted. This had been a large factory in which the Germans had made a courageous, if eventually ineffective, last stand.

In the afternoon the Brigade Padre — a Church of England priest — came round the camp. I never knew his name but, certainly whether living or dead, his memory deserves to be honoured. I remember him as a tall, stooping figure, good-humoured, cultured, always smiling and with a friendly word for all. At his side he carried a capacious bag from which he distributed what seemed to be an inexhaustible flow of Woodbines and journals, among which *John Bull* and *Answers* were prime favourites. His appearance, unheralded and unassuming, was ever welcome and his popularity was by no means limited by the religious beliefs of his beneficiaries. I was told, and experience was later to confirm, that he was in the habit of turning up in the unlikeliest places and was not afraid of wandering in the trenches on his own.

During the next night a shell fell in the camp near a bivouac, slightly wounding one of the occupants who was sent back to the dressing station for attention. On the following evening, after a day of rain, there was a second rather more serious accident as a number of men crowded round a fire to dry their sodden clothes. One man had foolishly put a Mills bomb detonator in one of his pockets. It exploded wounding him in the side and another in the hand. Both casualties went back, envied as only the rich are envied in civil life.

This had been a terrible day. The rain was cold, as autumn rain can be, and the bivouac incapable of dealing with such a downpour. Not only did water drip through in many places but the atmosphere was saturated. As I wrote the indelible pencil smeared across the pages. This was a dreary camp in any case. We had no washing facilities; the sanitary arrangements were primitive to say the least. By evening the whole area was fast becoming a latrine, while everything out of the rain was caked with mud.

That afternoon as I sat writing a letter home — no easy feat in the circumstances, but we grew accustomed to writing in the most difficult conditions — I could not help contrasting the depressing present with the pictures that the folks at home were given of the war. Tomorrow, we knew, we were going back into the trenches. At home they would be quite incapable of visualizing anything so frightful, even had we the freedom and the power of the pen to depict it. To be alive and yet feel oneself already dead, to be wet and cold and without any amenities, to be bound to a machine, unfree, comfortless, miserable and alone — that was how I felt. The loneliness when so many were involved is perhaps the least understandable today. We were too wrapped each in his personal misery, too intent upon his own personal world, to pay much attention to his neighbour's. The sense of abandonment was total.

Before we set out for the trenches on 27th October, whale oil was issued to grease our feet as a preventative of trench feet. It was evil-smelling stuff the immediate effect of which was to make one's feet feel colder, so we were generally dilatory in using it and resisted the orderlies who came to apply the treatment.

During the day our burden had been further increased with personal issues of Mills bombs, Very lights and other portable ammunition. As a result my load, in addition to the normal equipment, ammunition, rifle, overcoat, waterproof, two gas helmets and a steel helmet, included a shovel, two Mills bombs, two Very lights, a ground flare, a smoke bomb, a day's rations, leather jerkin, cap comforter, pair of leather trench gloves joined by a long tape, two sandbags and one hundred extra rounds of ammunition. All these were necessaries in that war but, looking back, it is incredible that we were able to transport so much under the conditions that prevailed.

The ground was heavy underfoot, but fortunately we were able to keep on top and maintain a straight line of march instead of being submitted to the meanderings of a trench. All seemed to be going smoothly as we rounded the far corner of High Wood when the screech of an approaching shell caused the laborious line to scatter. Two heavy shrapnels burst in the air above, squirting their death-dealing pellets into the mud around us. Two men fell and two more graves would have to be dug hard by that sombre wood. The line hurried forward, more than one of us mumbling a heart-felt prayer. My own fears were heightened at the thought of further bursts of those terrifying missiles.

We were now leaving the wood behind and trailing across broken ground towards the area of greater activity. On the ridge ahead heavy German 5.9s were hammering mercilessly and it looked as though we should have to brave the barrage. Between us and the ridge one of our planes had fallen in flames. Many figures were moving amid the lurid glow which threw long red shadows across the broken ground. Acclimatized as I was now to the idea of sudden and horrible death this infernal scene was almost too unreal to be believed. Yet the situation suddenly changed as the head of the file began to climb the final slope: almost miraculously the bombardment ceased and even the crackling bonfire seemed to be dying away behind us.

The company found its position in reserve in a trench known as Drop Alley. In front of us was a low rise behind which lay the shattered village of Flers, which had been captured when tanks were used for the first time. Our trench cut across towards the ridge while others zigzagged to left and right. Towards the horizon further to the right there was a fringe of trees with rolling country just discernible beyond. Somewhere on this side of the trees the Germans were entrenched and in that direction shells were continually bursting.

In our vicinity all was now quiet. There was little movement except for the occasional bobbing just above ground-level of a steel helmet as its owner moved across a shallow part of a trench. Occasionally a figure rose rapidly out of the ground and ran across the open to cut off a corner, a foolish proceeding in any case since, apart from its immediate hazard, such movement might identify our positions to the enemy. All around us, as far as one could see, the earth was churned into a continuous sea of mud, pock-marked with shell holes and littered with the pathetic debris of war. The whole landscape was of one colour — a dirty brownish grey. An occasional shell droned over in our direction to burst uselessly in the sludge. Such was the aspect of the particular corner of the vast Somme battlefield to which we were now being introduced.

As usual Jimmy and I were unlucky in our search for shelter. The few dug-outs had already been commandeered by our betters. We found a spot in the trench which was narrow and afforded good shelter, and there carved out a ledge sufficiently deep to allow two to sleep side by side. Earth still projected over the top and we covered the opening with a groundsheet. Actually this was a most dangerous arrangement and it shows the serious lack of interest of the officers that we were allowed to make do in this way. Our improvised shelter did in fact last for a while, affording us some protection from the cold autumn air between sentry turns.

By this time I was becoming used to taking the rum ration and even looking forward to its arrival, although its warming effects were short-lived. One night Jimmy managed to get two rations which made him delirious for he was as little used to strong drink as I was. He gabbled incoherently about friends at home and at one stage attempted to clamber over the parapet in search of Fritz. I had to force him back into our funk hole, making a mental note of the danger of such Dutch courage as drink could induce; in normal times Jimmy was the mildest of men.

Those nights were tedious and cold. Frequently the skies, behind both the enemy lines and our own, were lit up with the glow of burning dumps which had been ignited by shell-fire constantly probing for a target. Both sides must have lost a great deal of *materiel* in this way.

During the day we were kept busy tidying up the trench or in merely trying to look busy, for there was little scope for improvement with the resources at our disposal. Occasionally working parties were detailed, in which we two were invariably included. One afternoon we were sent to Flers village to bring back duckboards which had been dumped there. Duckboards consisted, of two lengths of timber joined by slats at close intervals of suitable width to make a dry track over the mud at the bottom of trenches. It was a weird deserted place, especially at that time of day, dominated by the abandoned tank looking ridiculous in its early demise, but not more ridiculous — or exasperated — than we felt trying to balance upon our shoulders an unwieldy length of duckboarding and to retain our balance as we crossed the shell-torn ground. We could hardly be expected to see the Punch-like humour of the scene at the time, and to make matters worse we were admonished on our way for exposing ourselves by a wandering red-hatted staff officer who chose that particular moment to turn up unexpectedly, as was their custom. He warned us about a sniper who had been at work in the neighbourhood and had had his successes. He did not stop to tell us how we could have collected these objects from an exposed dump and then transported them along a narrow trench without exposing ourselves.

On another occasion I went with a carrying party to fetch water from a dump by High Wood. At a water-point there a number of petrol tins filled with water had been stacked ready for transportation. Naturally we took this opportunity to quench our thirst for, despite the soddenness of everything, water was a scarce commodity and it was difficult to get enough to drink. Invariably the water was strongly flavoured with petrol — difficult to eliminate from the cans —

sometimes so powerfully as to be undrinkable. On the way we had a stroke of luck in finding a small supply of biscuits and jam, evidently dumped in the trench by a carrying party that had scuttled in a hurry. We hastened to expropriate as much as we could carry before its proper guardians came back to retrieve it.

Our cans of water were destined for the company's cookhouse, a large sandbagged shelter dug into the side of the trench. Although its sandbagged roof was supported by girders, no one could doubt that only the lightest enemy shell would be required to cut short our hot food supply. Not that this was more than lukewarm when it reached our part of the trench. Bacon was served with tea for breakfast. It was cold by the time we got it and generously sprinkled with mud that had slid down from the trench side. The tea invariably left a mud sediment in the bottoms of our mess tins.

All that day it rained intermittently and that night, as was to be expected, our primitive shelter at last fell in. Fortunately neither of us was sheltering at the time. At this juncture Jimmy and I were detailed for another water-carrying party. The night was pitch and the trenches now impassable; in places the duckboards floated like rafts. We slithered and floundered along the rim of the trench, having to jump across at places and soon becoming irretrievably lost. The Corporal in charge decided that the mission was impossible and we floundered back with difficulty, arriving eventually to discover that we had missed the rum ration. No one thought of putting by our share.

Despite the rain, which continued the following day, work in the trench was maintained and thus we continued, wet to the skin, cold and hopeless, wondering how long we could stand the aquatic bombardment. During the afternoon the enemy added to our discomforts by shelling the trench. A number of casualties went back. This incident was hardly surprising considering the movement above ground since our arrival, not all of it absolutely necessary. Nevertheless the latrines, in this case in a shell hole some yards from the trench, had to be approached over the top. Unfortunately these conveniences earned the reputation of death traps so that the trench itself was too often used instead. In the present instance, on the occasion of one of my visits, a shell had partially disinterred the body of a Tommy who had been fortunate enough to receive some sort of burial a few paces away from the improvised convenience.

On the last day of the month we moved forward to the Flers Line support trench. This was in places so deep in mud as to be almost impassable. The best shelter Jimmy and I could find was a sandbagged cover over a shelf upon which there was just room for us to sit side by side with our legs dangling into the trench. The previous occupants had fixed a curtain of empty sandbags to flap down in front at night and keep the cold air from blowing in their faces. This shelter was on the wrong side of the trench, facing the enemy, but we were still far enough back not to need worry a lot about this. As it happened we were fortunate in this situation as, not far back from the parados against which we leant, a battery of field guns had been dug in. When they fired, the blast from their muzzles drove down into the trench and not infrequently a premature burst sprinkled the parapet in front of us with venomous shrapnel bullets. We had to crouch down on the near side to evade the scaring pellets. No one took any notice of our plight, after all, we had not been assigned to the shelter — there was no apparent alternative. There was a strong element of free enterprise in the organization of our company.

As usual there was the inevitable alternation of sentry duties
and carrying parties — everything had to be carried, water,
duckboards, rations. There was unbounded opportunity to
think but little opportunity to rest, even had conditions
permitted. The food was poor. We were tired, hungry, cold and
often wet, but worse even than all this, we laboured under a
sense of injustice. One night Jimmy and I were turned out
twice for carrying parties. Protest was useless. Most of the
platoon were specialists, so-called — bombers, machine-
gunners, observers, snipers — all with good claims for
avoiding their share of fatigue duties. A caste system had been
built up. The old hands openly boasted that they had done
their turn and claimed that it was only right that the burden
should be passed to the newcomers, late participants in the
fighting — for so it may have appeared at the time. I might
have been convinced of the justness of this claim had I really
felt that all the men had earned the privilege they claimed, but I
knew they had not. There were habitual slackers among them,
'scroungers' who were making profit from the reputation of
the mutilated and the dead.

Returning from one of those agonizing and tedious jaunts in
the clammy dark night, we blundered past a party of the
Durham Light Infantry laden with pickets and barbed wire on
their way forward for a wiring job, who told us that a few
nights before on a similar mission they had suffered heavy
casualties. Such news of tragedy always brought heavier
depression upon our spirits. Despite the constant drumming
and flashing of the guns it was only now and again that the
hand of death stretched into one's own vicinity. The battlefield
most of the time was so impersonal, so distant. The near
picture was usually a conglomerate of drabness and physical
discomfort; yet we knew from the wings of rumour or the

measured procession across the stage of a stretcher party, that all around us, just beyond the range of our personal vision, horrible things were happening to someone just like ourselves. We lived in a state of continuing suspense.

On one occasion we went on a ration-carrying party to the forward troops and for the first time I found myself in the front line. It was quite unlike anything I had imagined. The journey up had been bad enough, for the communication trench was in a shocking state and we had to keep to it in this zone of immediate contact where any detected movement would draw fire. At one place I slipped into water up to my waist, a bad enough experience in the daytime but particularly upsetting in the cold night hours. We struggled to our destination, realising full well how those others, even worse off than ourselves, were depending upon us for their food.

The front line turned out to be little more than a shoulder-high ditch with no proper defence works. A shell had burst only recently, killing one of the defenders whose body lay shrouded by the parapet. The barren, shattered branches of a dead tree loomed ghost-like in the falling darkness, and we had to stoop low beneath girders and sandbags which bridged the trench at several points. At intervals the defenders were standing to, their eyes searching the gloom in front of them, at that moment not illuminated by enemy lights. Over all hung a brooding, sinister silence broken only by the squelch of our boots or a muttered curse as one of the carriers stumbled against some obstruction in the trench. Our mission fulfilled, were glad to get away from that land of horrible night, feeling some measure of gratitude that our situation was at least bearable.

On 3rd November we were back again in the bivouacs by High Wood, having been relieved by the 5th Northumberland

Fusiliers and withdrawn to the reserve trench on the previous afternoon. Before quitting the trench, which under the stress of the weather had considerably deteriorated since our first visit, Jimmy had a visitor. A devout Roman Catholic he was taken aside by his chaplain for a private talk. When he returned he was very subdued as though he had heard serious news, but he said nothing and I did not give the matter further thought.

It was in a way a relief to be back in the bivouacs: for, despite the muddy surroundings, here one could lie down and rest sheltered from the elements. At night, by packing close together, we could share some mutual warmth. In such a situation the least amenity was relative comfort, although in fact it was little enough. We remained unwashed and unshaven for there were no facilities even here. I was a veritable scarecrow, more dead than alive. My hands and forearms were badly cut by barbed wire and, in view of their almost permanent coating of drying mud, I wonder I did not get some kind of poisoning. But nature is very resistant in such circumstances and I do not remember that any one of us was incapacitated on this account. Our equipment too was in a shocking state. Caked with mud it was thrown to the foot of the bivouac in a heap and I do not recollect that anyone bothered about it at the time. Rifles were clogged, gas-masks were soaked and filthy and probably quite useless. We were certainly admonished to keep our rifles clean but in those conditions the task was hopeless and I doubt whether as a body we would have been capable of offensive action had it been required of us.

I had noted some relaxing of tension in our personal relations, although there was little to distract our thoughts from the gloomy possibilities of the immediate future. We certainly came to know our hard-bitten colleagues a little better, but I doubt whether in the mass they improved much on closer acquaintance. Serious conversation, when it rarely occurred, was centred round some such topic as the taking of prisoners. Most of our northern compatriots were against the practice, much to my dismay. Fritz, they insisted, did not take any, why should we? I did not really believe them though of course in such anarchy anything was possible. Lurid yarns were told of German prisoners who failed to reach the cages for some reason or other. The favoured tale was of a party of warlike Gurkhas who were extremely annoyed at having been detailed for such a time-wasting job as conducting a batch of prisoners to the rear. They discovered a short cut of their own and the authorities had turned a blind eye. Whether true or not the tale was received with satisfaction as an instance of rough justice. There were other stories of similar bloodthirstiness and rather more verisimilitude. There was, for example, the constantly recurring story of the unpopular officer shot in the back by his own men during an advance. Sergeant-majors in particular, a much-hated tribe, were commonly the subject of such yarns. There was little in such stories that was out of tune with realities, and if undoubtedly exaggerated in repetition, I should say there was more than a grain of truth in them. Their effect was sufficiently demoralizing to anyone with ideals.

The prevailing topic, however, overshadowing all else in interest, was sex, or rather a form of lewdness that masked the underlying urgencies of the subject. On a minority of younger men like myself this invariably had an embarrassing effect. Lacking actual experience, we still interpreted the urges that we could not understand in an idiom of romance which, supported by our religion, enabled us to free our minds from the desperate realities of the present and to dream of better, happier things. Yet if we resented the down-to-earth attitudes of our companions this did not prevent our listening with almost indecent interest to the tales that we deplored or joining with enthusiasm in the filthy doggerels which every soldier learns from constant repetition. The one most popular among the company was a humourless dirge which began, 'I love my wife, I love her dearly...' and then went on to catalogue all those parts of her anatomy to which this possessive love was attributed.

On the night of 4th November we were ordered to stand to from 10.00 p.m., which meant that we had to be ready to move out at a moment's notice to cope with any emergency. The Durhams and the Australians were to attack early the following morning. All the guns opened out during the night and my mind was divided between imagining the horror being suffered at that very moment by the men who were the main actors in the terrible but commonplace drama, and fear of the probable consequences to ourselves should our services be called upon. The following morning, when the artillery activity had subsided to a desultory though still lively bombardment, we were taken out on a working party on the roads and promptly lost in the process by the officer in charge. Certainly map-reading was not one of the outstanding accomplishments of the gentlemen leaders of the New Army.

This was a day of tension. All whom we met — and on that road everyone was to be met — had tales of terrible battle and disaster to those taking part. Reports as to whether the objectives had been taken or not were contradictory. Some spoke of complete failure, others of tactical success, but all were agreed on the heaviness of the casualties which was sufficiently evidenced by the streams of wounded coming back through the dressing stations. Over the company hung an air of tension while the state of emergency continued.

Early the following morning the call came, at least to some of us. I was awakened by furious rappings on the bivouac and general hullabaloo in the camp. 'Come on, get out, show a leg!' We thought it was a general stand-to. The sergeant-major, blear-eyed and angry, pounced upon me as I crawled from my sleep. 'You, you, get ready at once for a stretcher-bearing party: steel helmet, respirators, haversacks and no arms.' 'Come on, look lively, you buggers!' The number required was soon made up. Jimmy and I realised how silly we had been, as usual. The cute old hands had continued to snore. A quarter of an hour later a meagre meal was issued and we set out.

The morning was cold and wet: the drizzle continued as we filed along the light railway track towards the line. Heavy clouds hung low in the sky. The battle area was held in a clammy grip of inactivity, literally washed out by the elements. It was uncomfortable, but the rain at least had the virtue of protecting us from observation and shell-fire. We approached a low ridge and a line of trees where, the guide told us, the dressing station was situated. Heavy shells falling away to the right made us hurry as the path turned into a sort of cutting. Just here a pile of shattered brickwork marked the remains of a small hamlet with the delightful name of Eaucourt l'Abbaye, as shown by the inevitable notice board. A little further on we came upon the cabin and shelters that formed the dressing station, in what seemed a very exposed position and under a row of tall old trees, which had suggested its name of 'Seven Elms'.

An RAMC man immediately selected a small group of us to form the first party — it included me but not Jimmy — and led us back to the shattered village where we veered right and made towards a hump-like eminence in the middle distance, which we came to know as the Butte de Warlencourt. This mound seemed literally to dominate the area and, although I did not realise it at the time, was one of the key positions in the battle-line. It had already been the objective of many attacks and counter-attacks.

Other indications all about us as we filed forward conveyed a story of ceaseless battle in which we were now to be sort of guest participants. Out of the endless mud parts of human bodies protruded, reminding me of a highly coloured picture of Dante's Inferno which I had seen as a child. Despite the insistent horror of the surrounding reality my personal vision contributed its own ingredients to a nightmare, and if this is not easily comprehensible in the seventies it must not be forgotten that the world which had been shattered for us in 1914 was one in which sudden death and destruction were regarded as in the very nature of things abnormalities. The carrying party was passing through a shambles. Here a hand clutched up out of the mud, there a head half submerged in the filth exposed only the black hair. I shuddered as I narrowly avoided stepping on the ghastly pink hindquarters of another unfortunate.

More immediate and forceful terror intervened to cut short my contemplation of that horrible sepulchre. A salvo of enemy shells drove us helter-skelter into the trench, which we had been skirting for the sake of speed. We were only just in time. The whole area was again swept by a tornado of fire that threatened the very existence of the trench and promised to add us as a further quota to the charnel house. This was clearly a hot quarter but fortunately for us the winding trench soon led out of the immediate focus of fire.

Turning a bend we were, in startling contrast, confronted by a very different sight, a sight so amazing that for a brief spell all fear was driven from our minds. The sides of the trench were cluttered with ration bags containing bread, bully, jam, pork and beans, Maconochies (tins of vegetables mixed with a little meat), biscuits, even chocolate and cigarettes, presumably intended for the officers since we did not see this sort of ration in the line. Evidently a ration party traversing this terror-stricken zone had only recently been caught in the barrage and had decamped ignominiously, leaving their burdens and the men in the front line to get on as best they could. Instinctively reacting to this marvellous sight we forgot our mission and threw ourselves upon the rations, intent upon assuaging the hunger that was never far away. Unfortunately there was little that could be eaten without some preparation and our carrying capacity was limited. I grabbed a bag crammed with tins of jam, before the NCO, who was quite unconcerned by the immorality of our depredations, hurried us away from the miniature El Dorado.

Shortly thereafter the trench tailed away into a waste of shell-holes situated some hundred yards or so on this side of the Butte which now dominated the scene. Heavy shells were pounding the intervening ground and we had no alternative but to run the gauntlet. The bag of jam became a dead weight that threatened to hold me down to the target like a fly on sticky paper. Added to which the ground was just a quagmire. I flung my treasure trove from me and struggled frantically towards the shelter of the mound, which rose up, a cliff of earth from the plain, forming a sheltered pocket into which an enemy missile would have to be nicely aimed to penetrate. We were instructed to wait there while the RAMC man proceeded into a trench leading round the right-hand side of the mound towards the front positions.

This welcome respite enabled us to collect our senses and, with the aid of our jack-knives, to satisfy our hunger on the rations that had been salvaged. The Butte completely obscured any view forward but acted as a most effective screen for us. Shells continued to burst on the top or, just missing it, to slide over with a screech and burst fifty or sixty yards away filling the air with flying muck and metal. So resilient is the human mind and easily inured to the impossible that amid the horror we sat round like a picnic party, merely crouching closer to the ground each time a shell skimmed over. We had a feeling of safety now that was probably not justified by the actual screening capacity of the Butte. Khaki-clad figures lay sprawled in death about the foot of the mound which bore all the signs of recent fierce conflict. A couple of yards from where I squatted lay the huddled figure of a young man shot through the head. In retrospect I am surprised at my callousness in thus being able to enjoy a snack in the presence of horrifying death.

We had to wait for some time. Our resting minds were given plenty of opportunity to consider fearfully the probabilities of our own contribution to this tragedy. At last stretcher parties began to arrive along the trench. It was to be our task to act as relays on the final stage back to the dressing station. Four men were assigned to each stretcher and there was no question of our using the trench. If cowardice had been lethal I should have died on the spot at the mere prospect of returning across that zone of death. Annihilation now seemed inevitable and pre-ordained. No further dallying was to be tolerated; the stretcher parties moved at intervals. I happened to be assigned to the last stretcher, not the most acceptable position in such a procession. Our man, poor devil, was a bad case who groaned at every step.

A miracle now happened. The shelling stopped for the first time since we had reached the Butte. The weight was heavy but with four to share the burden the task was not insupportable.

What created the main difficulty was the shocking state underfoot. We did all we could to keep the stretcher level but it was impossible. As one or another stepped into a shell-hole causing us to stumble at different angles, the stretcher tipped and tossed like a ship at sea. Our man cried out in pain and cursed us for our clumsiness, not realising the true reason for it. We relieved our own feelings by cursing him in turn for an ungrateful hound.

But we pressed forward. The air around us seemed literally to vibrate with the threat of another barrage and I listened apprehensively for the approach of shells. Standing up as we were, four men with a loaded stretcher at shoulder height, we seemed to dominate the terrible landscape and to invite instant annihilation. Nothing happened. We gained the surer ground alongside the trench without mishap and the line of stretchers advanced methodically and surely towards the haven where the wounded would be succoured and we should find safety.

Suddenly a new danger materialized. A rifle shot rang out and a bullet droned over followed by more. An enemy sniper was firing at us. Anger overwhelmed our fears as we pressed forward. Another shot and I saw the stretcher just ahead lurch as one of the bearers slipped to the ground, dead. It was young Janes of our draft and of the old Hertfordshires; the bullet had pierced a vital spot in his groin. 'Into the trench,' shouted my companions as the marksman turned his attention to us. He worked more quickly than we could. One bullet struck the ground between our feet, a second hit the earth a yard or so in front and a third droned by. By this time we had managed to lower our burden to the ground and scuttle into the trench. I felt some compunction at leaving the poor fellow above ground, but he presented a much more difficult target there than when we held him high in the air.

We waited a little while, discussing this unexpected incident angrily. Over on the ridge there was a row of trees and we concluded that the sniper was hidden in one of them, possibly behind our front positions, for the Germans made a practice of leaving behind marksmen when they had to withdraw. While we could excuse the impartiality and anonymity of the artillery barrage we had none for this man firing upon an unarmed party whose mission of mercy was too obvious to be misunderstood. Even in the midst of such horrible bloodshed this action was a clear instance of murder.

After a few stunned minutes the situation began to take charge of us again. We had to get on. Lifting our burden with a great effort, for it seemed to have gained weight in that period of tension, we pressed forward. The tenseness continued and so did the quiet until we were approaching Eaucourt l'Abbaye, where we were passed by the remainder of our group on their way out. We warned them about the sniper. As it turned out they were to get off less lightly than ourselves. Already the barrage had resumed and shells were falling all around. We had to manhandle the stretcher across the trench and our man was unavoidably jolted. To an accompaniment of his heart-rending cries and the bursting of shells in the vicinity we pressed on in haste to the dressing station, feeling that everything justified our thus hurrying towards the place of comparative safety. Here we were instructed to stand by for further orders.

A long row of stretcher cases awaited attention, sheltered by the low cutting. Some were taking things hardly — and who could blame them? — others recognizing their good fortune were behaving with the greatest restraint and *sang froid* despite smashed limbs and grievous wounds. To most a cigarette was a real solace, while the mere thought of leaving this dreadful place was sufficient to mitigate their discomfort and fears.

They laughed and joked and I, poor bedraggled Tommy that I was, could not refrain from envying them their 'Blighties'. Alas, it is to be feared that many were too far gone to reach that haven.

We waited throughout the remainder of that terrible day for orders that, fortunately for us, never came. Shells continued to fall, the medical men to labour at their work unconcernedly and without haste. Stretchers bearing those who had received attention were loaded on the light railway which was to convey them smoothly to the rear. As we loitered under cover of the cutting beneath the broken elms I found it difficult to understand why this forward dressing station had not been discovered by the enemy gunners and blown to hell. It was in a very exposed and very advanced position for such an activity.

At nightfall I was assigned as one of the man-propellers of the trucks on the railway and undertook this new task with heartfelt relief. When we reached hutments at the terminus of the line where the stretchers were transhipped for the next stage of their journey I was astonished to receive from the RAMC men, as a sort of recompense for the day's work, a half loaf and a complete tin of Maconochie, intended as a ration for two. It should have been warmed up but one could not be fussy under those conditions. It was sufficiently palatable cold, if indigestible, and I finished it with most of the bread, a truly gargantuan meal at any time. I was feeling thoroughly ill by the time I arrived at the bivouacs. No doubt I deserved to be, though perhaps there were extenuating circumstances.

We continued for a few more days undertaking working parties in the same position. It was relatively comfortable, compared with the trenches and although this was in the zone of the lighter heavies the Germans' retaliatory fire was not too serious. There were more promising targets among the dumps a little further back. One day we spent propelling waggons loaded with materials to one of the winter quarters being constructed by the Royal Engineers. It was a very wet day and we were fortunate to be able to shelter for much of the time in one of the completed huts where our RE boss had a brazier alight. To have access to this warmth was a real treat amidst all our current hardships. There was a good deal of yarning interspersed with singing. The favourite ditty that day was about a certain Casey Jones. It was a lugubrious dirge of numerous verses, such as:

> Casey Jones riding on his Engine
> Casey Jones with a Banana in his Hand
> Casey Jones stopped a German Whizz-bang
> Now he's pushing Daisies up in No Man's Land.

These could be varied *ad lib* and suited to the particular occasion, but their drift provided epitaphs for the many Casey Jones's who gave their lives for an ideal in the years around 1916. At the time, with death in our minds and its visual evidence all about us, there was nothing incongruous in the enthusiasm with which the refrain was taken up by all. I could not help envying those RE their cosy hut and also their light-heartedness.

We were soon back in the trenches, proceeding from Prue Trench forward again to Flers Switch and falling into the routine of fatigues and trying, not usually with much success, to keep dry. The cooks sent up a concoction of rice with raisins, well mixed with sandbag fibres, which was so revolting to many of my companions that they would not touch it, though I can scarcely imagine they had been so pampered in peace to justify such squeamishness. I decided that hungry men could not be epicures and did full justice to this lukewarm mess as a change from the normal bully-beef stew flavoured with Somme mud. It was in fact an addition rather than a substitute.

It was at this time that I first noticed a new pain in my feet. It started as a dull ache that seemed to be deep inside, and soon became agonizing. I did not know it then but I was suffering the first symptoms of trench feet. My feet were cold and clammy yet there was nothing to show. Consequently I said nothing, for I feared beyond all else being accused of malingering. I doubt if it would have made any difference had I reported sick. The medical people were so used to malingering that they had grown callous to anything that could not be easily tested. Yet a little attention at this early stage might have put matters right. In more than one sense I did not realise what I was in for.

One afternoon a party of us had what was at that time an unusual experience. The rain had ceased and light mists wreathed the trenches, reducing visibility to almost zero. An enemy plane swooped down and swept our stretch of trench with machine-gun fire. Fortunately such tactics were still untried and the attack on this occasion was ineffectual. A momentary spinal chill and the consciousness of a new threat to our existence were the net effects as far as I was concerned.

Late on the night of 12th November we were ordered forward to dig a trench a short way back from and parallel to the front line. The night was pitch. Heavy clouds loured in the sky and it was only then the enemy sent up a light that we could see more than a few paces in any direction. In fact it was a good night for a secret operation of this sort, but the ground was so water-logged that below two to three feet water immediately seeped into the bottom of our new construction. It was a hopeless, exasperating task and our position was far from comfortable. From the placing of the enemy rockets we learned that his line was not far beyond our own positions, and whenever a rocket came over lower than usual with a more acute trajectory we were lit up as a group of petrified figures standing in grotesque attitudes, motionless lest movement should disclose our presence. The noise too of picks and shovels inexpertly handled seemed almost certain to give us away. But the watchers too — though one always endowed them with superhuman wakefulness — inevitably had plenty to occupy their minds. In all probability any unusual movement, in that night of changing cloud-shapes, merely made that part of the Somme battlefield assume an even more than usual Walpurgis Night aspect.

Now and again a burst of machine-gun or rifle fire caused us to crouch low. But such enemy action was not the worst of the night's hazards. We worked on and on under the tireless energy of the NCOs who wanted to get the job done and knew that there were slackers among us, even in such a situation. Slacking, almost a religion with a certain type, was a senseless form of non-cooperation which did nothing but lengthen the suffering of all. The night grew steadily colder and to our other discomforts thirst was an added torment. I felt my last strength running out with every swing of the shovel, while my feet were now very painful. Just nearby, at the back, was a large shell-hole which had become a miniature pond. As a light glimmered across its surface one thought of unimaginable refuse in its depths. Yet many went without hesitation to drink. Unable to restrain myself any longer and with thoughts of the dead bodies that so often lay in such holes, I took out a small collapsible aluminium cup which I had brought out from home and scooped up some of the mud-polluted water. Even as I drank, a reflecting light seemed to pick out pink streaks across the surface of the pond. The water tasted of chemicals but that did not prevent new life from streaming into my body.

The night's experience seemed to have given a final jerk to my indisposition. When I awoke next morning from a sleep of exhaustion I not only ached in every limb but my feet were extremely painful. They were swollen now, but otherwise did not look abnormal. Then the blow fell, although in my own private pain I hardly realised at first just what it meant. We were to go forward that night to lie in close support of an attack which the other companies of the battalion would launch the following day. This seemed an incredible plan in view of all the existing conditions and the poor state of the company at the end of such a protracted spell without rest or proper shelter. If I had my own special indisposition at that moment I was certainly not blind to the fact that there was not a man among us fit to face up to such an ordeal.

That morning a Medical Officer came round the trenches to pick out the unfit and sent them back for treatment. He looked cursorily at my feet, murmured something to his orderly who made an entry in his notebook, and informed me that I should receive instructions later to go back. I received this information with a mixture of relief and sorrow. It seemed wrong to miss the attack when the others had to go through with it. Jimmy Downs, Bryant and Taylor, in the same bay with me, had no doubts as to the rightness of the decision, and their kindness I shall never forget.

Throughout that long day I lived in two worlds and seemed to be nursing a split personality. I was no longer frightened by the ordeal ahead, but moved by an intense sorrow for those who had to face it. Naturally I felt great compassion for Jimmy, the significance of whose recent conversation with the Roman Catholic padre I now understood. While there had been plenty of rumours of an attack since we had come in, it was now clear that the authorities had known for some time that we had a special ordeal ahead of us. I was specially affected by the fact that during these last few days Jimmy and I, who had been such good friends and companions, had somehow become estranged. It was one of those indefinite misunderstandings that arise when so many are thrown haphazardly into each other's company. This day at least was something of a day of reconciliation. My own good fortune was tempered by a strong feeling on my part that my indisposition ought not to be considered a blessing in disguise. It was not in the same category as a wound inflicted by the enemy. I felt a certain meanness at thus evading my responsibilities even though I could hardly be blamed for what had happened to me. Yet the indefatigable kindness of my near companions soothed my mental anguish. I had done little enough to deserve their generosity.

The day wore on to the accompanying preparations for battle. Ammunition was checked and adjusted, additional stretcher-bearers appeared with new white armlets marked boldly with a red cross. There was a purposeful bustling that foreshadowed a much more serious undertaking than our previous experience at Le Sars. Yet it all seemed to be happening in a world to which I no longer belonged. I had no doubts whatever that instructions from authority would eventually arrive — until the approach of evening. Then I came back to reality with a jolt. A badly-stricken stretcher case was sent away. Final instructions were passed along the trench. The NCO carrying them knew nothing of orders to evacuate anyone else. His instructions applied to us all. My companions indignantly protested. They decided to take me to company headquarters, which they did, half dragging me. I cried out with pain every time my feet touched the ground.

At the dug-out they inquired for an officer, but a sergeant, half drunk with rum, came out and glared at me. I knew at once that my plaint would be hopeless and the horror of the position invaded my mind. I told him what the medical orderly had said. He swore. No orders would come up now. I should go in with the rest, and rightly too. I was swinging the lead, a coward. My feet were not bad: everybody's feet were bad. Clear out. Other NCOs came out and backed him up. It was all too much for me and I broke down in tears.

The emotional collapse was soon followed by an overwhelming feeling of anger at the injustice of the accusation. What happened to those men, who were so obviously not equal to their responsibilities, I do not know. Almost certainly some were to be killed, but were I to meet any who may have survived I would not know them. Their personalities were completely vague even at the time. Against their callousness I contrasted the generous indignation of my helpers, who now had no other recourse but to assist me painfully back to the trench.

I now had to face the new, totally unexpected situation. Looking back I cannot now feel that the sergeant's reaction was altogether unreasonable. He did not know the facts — though of course he should have and in a properly organized unit would have known — but he did know that we were all frightened to death and that he had to be on his guard against every subterfuge. His real fault was that he and his companions were tipsy at a moment of such grave responsibility and that he was therefore incapable of considering objectively whether or not I might be a menace to the safety of my companions in my present state. His fault was aggravated by the fact that his additional rum ration could only have accrued through his purloining more than his due share of the official issue — as indeed commissioned officers and NCOs almost invariably did. The agony of my feet was not patent to anyone but myself. As it was, it took me half an hour to edge my swollen feet into my boots and this had to be done with Jimmy's help. I can sense that pain now as I can remember the compassion of those about me who knew the truth.

Some advised me to get to the dressing station at once, others to see an officer at all costs, but I was now too discouraged and undecided to do anything. Dark night had fallen: all preparations had now been made. Time seemed to have come to a halt. I struggled with my problem but the fear of cowardice was now uppermost in my mind. I knew I was a coward, without my disability. I could see a truth in my own mind, things that my companions could barely discern, except as images of their own fears.

It must have been past midnight when the order came for us to fall in. I had to be dragged up from the trench and, as I stood in the ranks swaying on my feet, I used my rifle as a crutch. The NCO called the roll in the dim light of a hand lantern. Neither he nor his companions were sober nor was the officer when he arrived to take over. This was not a normal situation, fortunately for the reputation of the British army.

I was still undecided, fear grappling with pride within me, when my companions literally pushed me forward to restate my case. It was no use. The officer spoke incoherently, laughed foolishly and moved away flashing his torch among the gathered ranks. Jimmy strongly advised me to go to the dressing station, which we knew was not far off the route that we were to take. I promised to do so but was still in two minds. Apart from my disability I did not relish losing touch with my friends.

The platoon moved off. I hobbled along with them, still needing my rifle to maintain my balance. It was immediately evident that I could not keep up. The platoon drew ahead and I knew events were taking control. As the tail of the column disappeared into the darkness Jimmy shouted 'Good-bye and good luck', and I was alone. Obviously I must find the dressing station: it was my only hope. Fortunately my mind was clear and I knew the direction. Yet I stumbled forward so slowly and the time seemed so long that I began to have misgivings. Suddenly I discerned near at hand glimmers from the hutments at the side of the road. I hesitated for some minutes in the quiet night before I summoned courage to knock on the shutter.

An RAMC man answered and listened sympathetically to my plaint. Then he asked to see my ticket and when I told him I had nothing he replied that they were cleared for battle casualties and could not take anyone without a chit from his unit. He was sorry but could not act against orders. As my unit was attacking there would be a battalion dressing station where I should be well advised to report. He emphasized the precariousness of my position and I knew it would not be easy to meet a charge of desertion, which in such a situation on the field of battle could be summarily punished by death. Might I not make a most convenient sacrifice to strengthen the morale of the rest of the army? My informant knew that the headquarters of the 7th Northumberland Fusiliers was under the ridge by Pioneer Alley and directed me towards the light railway which would guide me in the right direction. I thanked him and he closed the door. Once again I was alone, wretched but no longer undecided. I had to follow the good advice I had just been given.

Thus I entered the second stage of the night's fearsome journey, a stage that stands out in my mind as if it happened yesterday. Recollecting my physical condition and the immeasurable weight of my fear, I cannot understand how I did what I did and retained my sanity. Imagine me, an insignificant and frightened youth with a less than fully active body out there in the black night of the Somme battlefield, which was simmering with the inaction that often preluded the storm of battle. Around me all was dark and deserted, or appeared deserted, for if there were waiting men not far away they were out of my sight and as quiet as the tomb. Away on the horizon shell-bursts indicated that the normal routines were taking place between the lines. The surrounding gloom and stillness held a menace of its own. I was so terrified that I could not have imagined fear being further intensified, whatever might happen. Yet I was only at the beginning of that night's happenings.

My progress was still slow, but now mental pain had gained the upperhand over physical pain and as my legs became accustomed to regular movement my pace quickened, until there was little more than a limp to suggest that there was anything wrong. With regulated steps the pain subsided, my mobility had been restored. I realized that so long as I kept moving I should be all right. I reached the railway track and knew I was on the right route. I saw no one until I came to a kind of siding where groups of men were busily unloading ammunition for the forthcoming barrage. They confirmed my direction and again I left the zone of human activity. Although I was following a well-used track the night was now so dense that I feared losing my way. In my loneliness I wanted to shout just to hear my own voice. Reality had become a dream, nightmare a fact.

Then, to add to my distress, the enemy began to shell the track ahead. Heavy shells burst now to right now to left. Shrapnel screamed and spanged into the ground. I crouched at each explosion, but as there was no cover I hurried forward as fast as I could. I could not run to relieve the tension. I felt like a maimed fly under a merciless but blind flail. Death must be inevitable. Yet I continued onwards because there was nothing else I could do.

The shelling stopped as suddenly as it had begun and within a few moments I stumbled into a shell-hole, the result of a direct hit on the road. The smell of explosives filled the air. No one using that particular sector of the track could have survived. The Germans would not have been pleased to know that all those shells had been expended on a road that was deserted except for one Tommy who had had the luck to escape their insensate shower of death. Had I been knocked out there my name would certainly have been registered among the missing who were never traced. Yet my heart seemed to lighten as I left the fatal spot behind. Even the most abject fear has its limits.

The route stretched ahead interminably. Time had halted to mock my puny strength. Yet it was indeed amazing that amid all the preparations going on around me I met no one. No doubt the road had been cleared by design. At last I heard voices and a party emerged from the darkness to cross the road ahead. I shouted to make sure that I did not miss them and after a brief pause the figure of an officer loomed out of the shadows. He confirmed that my objective was now only a short way down the road.

I soon reached the low ridge, along the lea of which a row of lights shone on the duckboard track from semi-circular dug-out entrances which faced away from the firing line. The track was bustling with runners and others making their final preparations. I came to an opening marked with a large red cross. Things looked very cosy within: a large fire burned brightly and on the step of the sandbagged doorway sat a sergeant-major looking very contented with life.

Quite by chance a Tommy entered just as I arrived on the scene. I drew back into the shadow. He seemed to be making some petition. There was a pause; then a scuffle as the private ran out, followed by the irate warrant officer uttering venomous imprecations against lead-swingers and cowards. What little courage I had summoned to make my own plea oozed away. I felt that the stranger's plight was probably just as bad as mine and that I could not again face that unfair charge. I may well have been wrong. Fatigued as I was I seemed to have no alternative but to continue to the forward position and accept what fate had in store for me. The question was whether I should arrive in time.

The entrance to Pioneer Alley, the main communication trench in this sector, led up by steps through the ridge. Shells were bursting above, while others, just missing the skyline, were sliding over to burst on the flat ground behind me. As I approached the gap, moving now with some difficulty up the slope, a dishevelled figure bearing a sack over his shoulder scampered down towards me shouting breathlessly that the entire trench was being heavily strafed. There was no alternative to running the gauntlet, for time was getting short. Fortunately the trench was deep, thrusting forward in wide zigzags and affording good cover. My eyes had become accustomed to the darkness and my range of vision was good considering the gloom. The trench sides were wet. Thick mud at the bottom pulled my feet causing the pain to return. I tried to skirt the spots where the mud lay deepest, hugging the trench side wherever it made a sharp turn, stretching as far as I could across the slimy pools in dark corners.

All of a sudden I blundered upon a fellow sufferer stuck helplessly in the mud. As he endeavoured to pull one leg free the other became more deeply embedded so that he was floundering hopelessly. He appealed to me piteously for help. I could now see crouching on the parapet an officer who urged him to get on while making not the least effort to assist him. They were taking up signalling instruments to the line. I knew at once that I had not the strength to help and the fear of getting bogged myself added wings to my retreat. Fortunately the shelling had stopped. I withdrew into the previous traverse and climbed where the trench was lowest laboriously to the surface. I was conscience-stricken at my lack of humanity, but after all the other man was not alone. I was now out of sight of the two men but I heard the officer threatening to shoot the soldier if he did not move on. Indignation was added to my confused feelings as I continued my way alongside the trench. What happened to those two anguished souls I do not know.

Around me now spread a wide expanse of undulating shell-pitted ground that sloped distantly to the horizon. I was released from the claustrophobia that had gripped me and in this new situation felt like a giant ambling above the world of men, whose proper habitat was below ground in the curling trench which continued to be my guide and landmark. Ahead I could see the enemy line, disclosed by the popping lights which lit up the landscape intermittently. Except for the subdued sound and the lights there was now little noise until I heard metallic digging near at hand.

As I approached I discerned a line of figures working feverishly on a new trench that led away to the left. This was C Company digging in a close support line for the forthcoming attack. I was hailed with a good deal of warmth and was told to work my way along to the left flank, where I found Corry, a Cumberland man, digging a funk-hole on his own. He immediately invited me to join him, which I was only too pleased to do. Corry had but recently come within the sphere of our friendship. Both Jimmy and I liked him, though he was perhaps a little taciturn and inclined to keep to himself. I suspect that he was glad to have a companion in facing the forthcoming ordeal. Certainly his solicitude saved my life.

Corry had worked to considerable effect, making a funk-hole which had a bank of earth some three to four feet deep at front and sides, backing on to the trench which was there about two feet deep, but dropped steeply on our left for a few yards before petering out into the waste that stretched away on our flank. This short sector was occupied by some of the company's NCOs. Obviously our position had the advantage of a swell in the ground for rightwards the trench was very shallow and the workers there had made much less progress than Corry towards achieving good cover. Moving like black gnomes in the night, all continued to work strenuously to improve the position. Jimmy and the two Yorkshiremen, Bryant and Taylor, were a few yards to our right. They had welcomed me as I came up.

Corry told me he had had a feeling I should turn up and he had planned his funk-hole on that assumption. He toiled doggedly with his spade while I did what I could to assist with my entrenching tool, though ineffectively. I felt thoroughly in the way and with the cessation of movement my feet were again painful. My good companion cursed me roundly for my clumsiness as I shuffled from side to side. Thus the night passed.

As dawn began to spread its first light across the sky the noise of digging died away: the whole line fell silent and still. Since the shelling of the communication trench, the night had been unusually quiet. Now there was a queer tension in the air. A sense of unreality possessed us as though we were disembodied witnesses of a drama over which we had no control yet desperately hoped it might prove a nightmare from which we would wake to more pleasant reality. And all the time we knew there could be no escape. Only those who have thus waited upon a grim death will understand that sickening emptiness of spirit as one murmurs to God a supplication for release from a terror fast becoming insupportable. The hour of madness was at hand.

The attack was timed to begin with daylight at 7.00 a.m. A few moments before the appointed hour a hoarse voice whispered 'It is time'. Crouching against our all-too-flimsy shield we waited, Corry and I.

Suddenly from behind us the storm broke with a thundering roar as the guns began to pump over their screaming missiles, high above our heads, towards the enemy positions. Once again death went riding in earnest across the weary battlefield of the Somme, and this time I was there.

Despite my terror the thought that I was at that moment on the very fringe of history seized my imagination and for a while recognition of my own personal agony receded into the depths of my consciousness. Surely this flail of death must sweep all before it, obliterating all enemy resistance? But retaliation was not slow in coming. A barrage of 5.9s fell about our positions shrouding the ground with acrid fumes. The earth trembled at their impact. My eardrums threatened to burst as the deadly flashes blazed near us, first in front, then behind, while in the air above ugly shrapnel bursts added to the horror. It was here that I first saw shrapnel shells with double bursts which the Germans were trying out at that time.

Screams from the wounded pierced the din, and dim crouching shapes of stretcher-bearers moved back and forth behind us. Out of the murk in front came a medley of noises — rifle fire, the rattle of machine-guns and the muffled roar of our own shells beating a regular tattoo about the enemy positions.

The bombardment continued, and it seemed doubtful whether anyone could survive. After the blind fury of the first response the enemy gunners settled down to more methodical ways. In full daylight the recent diggings were no doubt clearly visible to their observers. The situation became even more terrifying. Shells now came over in salvos, mathematically straddling the trench from front to rear, making it almost certain that at least one would register a hit or near miss. The line was being converted into a shambles. Fire, smoke, din, screams, stench, mud, blood, death; a ceaseless repetition that added up to hell. I felt that every shell was making straight for me. I crushed against our wall of earth, holding my breath as the rain of debris scattered over the funk-hole.

The stretcher-bearers were incredible in their courage, but their task was beyond human fulfilment. As the smoke cleared momentarily I saw two stretcher parties moving along the lip of Pioneer Alley over to our right. One party disappeared to earth as an enemy salvo threw up black fountains along the horizon; the other dissolved into oblivion under a direct hit. Volunteers were called for and later all who could help were ordered to assist. Corry went but fortunately was not called upon to run the gauntlet of the communication trench. I was saved by my feet.

Casualties mounted steadily. The NCOs on our left evacuated their position which, despite its apparent depth, was subject to enfilade from the broken ground on the flank. A stranger joined us in the funk-hole, his arm swathed in bloody bandages, with the intention of delaying his journey back until things quietened. Shortly afterwards the funk-hole in which Jimmy and the two Yorkshiremen were sheltering received a direct hit and only Jimmy was pulled clear. I saw him lying in the trench a few yards away and, despite my anguish, I could not suppress an instinctive feeling of envy. I did not realize how badly hurt he was.

I felt that I must go to him but fear of leaving our own frail shelter all but rooted me to the spot. I began to crawl towards the low heap of rubble that obstructed the trench, when another shell screeched down, enveloping the trench in a cloud of muck. A man was hurled over the parapet just in front of me, where he lay screaming pitifully. A sergeant came in from the far side and tried to drag the wounded man back from his exposed position but was unable to do so. A sprinkle of bullets came over the edge of the earthwork. The NCO now called for assistance, and I, frightened but impelled by a sense of duty that for the moment overcame all thought of self-preservation, crawled to the prostrate form. We hauled the wounded man down into the funk-hole. Severely injured, he was grateful for the water I was able to give him. Stretcher bearers came to tend him.

Meanwhile Jimmy had been carried away, so that I did not speak to him. All the events happened inconsequentially, leaving in my mind a series of disjointed pictures, the one element of continuity being contributed by the ceaseless beat of the guns and the racking terror that was magnified by my comparative inactivity. And now there was the thoughts of Jimmy to increase my confusion: Jimmy escaping from this hell, albeit at a price, into a different reality. I forgot the dangers of getting away, overlooked the pain, and envied him his good fortune.

My selfishness earned poignant censure when on the following day I learned that he had died before reaching the dressing station. The shock was such that for a time I could not believe. Jimmy so gentle and so decent, dead. I thought of all we had shared, and exaggerated to my discredit the misunderstanding that had lately arisen between us. And in my state of mind I was again to fail him who had been my friend. I was not to carry out the promise we had mutually exchanged to write to the other's relations in case of disaster. Yet it was not fear or unwillingness that made me fail in this duty, a dereliction I regret to this day. I could not bring myself to write the painful truth that would break the hearts of Jimmy's two gentle maiden aunts in Bromley. Neither had I the skill to write in such a way that the news might be softened for the recipients. Later, when I might have brought myself to attempt the sad assignment, I had lost the address with my other personal belongings.

The storm of fire continued throughout the morning and it is difficult to understand how any one of us could have escaped destruction. In the afternoon when an unreal stillness had settled over the battlefield orders for us to withdraw were shouted along the line. Corry and I were now right on the left flank and the last to go. We had to traverse the position from end to end. The sight was a ghastly one. The low, newly-dug trench and series of funk-holes had been so churned up that all evidence of human participation had been erased. Only our own funk-hole had escaped a direct hit and if our companions had sometimes escaped death or wounding it was because they had not remained in the one position throughout the battle. Bodies of the dead lay here and there, some gazing serenely at the sky, others in the distorted attitudes in which death had caught them. I recognized friends and some whom I had almost grown to regard as enemies. Among them was the spare Cockney bricklayer, whom I had come nearer to hating than anyone in all my life. His sarcastic face, his insults to the new draft, his successful attempts to evade his fair share of the working parties were now all things of the past. I could feel only an overwhelming pity for him as for all the others who had done nothing to merit such a horrible end.

Yet with death's handiwork so immoderately displayed all around I could not suppress a sort of triumphant wonder at my own immunity. The hour of terror had passed.

The remnants of the company were packed into a trench branching away on the far side of Pioneer Alley. It was deep and well hidden, and had not much suffered in the bombardment. It was now doubly evident why we had suffered so badly. Our newly dug and ineffective line had merely drawn fire. The only reason for having such a support line close behind our own front line was to have troops in a position to meet a counter-thrust by the enemy; probably the slope of the ground had suggested the need for such an arrangement. (Looking back it seems that the company had been uselessly sacrificed — another of the many occasions when lives had been needlessly squandered in that Great War.) In our new trench we saw the NCOs from the exposed trench on our left who had now joined the Sergeant-Major and the rest of the company staff in this much better protected position and were looking little the worse for our ordeal. I had much food for thought for the rest of the afternoon.

Our new location, though safer, proved most uncomfortable, for it was a thoroughfare for parties constantly passing backwards and forwards carrying instruments, testing wires, jostling us at every turn. Occasionally a shell burst nearby but this was of little account after the tornado of the morning. I was cold and weary, hungry and depressed. As my thoughts turned frequently to those who yesterday had been alive and now were no more, my own pains became insignificant. So many lives sacrificed for a few yards of useless ground that might well be wrested back at any moment. I thought with solicitude and envy of Jimmy whose fate I had yet to learn.

At stand-to a corporal scrambled along the trench bringing consternation in train. 'Come along, me lads,' he shouted, as though we were all aware of what was afoot. A few moved, but the majority just ignored the invitation. He stared at me and added 'You too.' Stilling my immediate impulse to mention my feet, I joined the line of protesting men. We collected boxes of bombs and thus laden set off for the new front line. The communication trench, no doubt formerly part of the German defence system, meandered across the terrain that until this morning had been no-man's-land. It was much battered and deep in mud but still a good trench, affording welcome cover for our errand. But the sticky bottom soon began to play havoc with my feet, which for a while had been quiescent. I found it difficult to lift them clear, but weakness from lack of rest would have largely accounted for this. In the gathering gloom the route seemed interminable. To and fro we zigzagged between wet clammy walls, though the distance, as the crow flies, could not have been great. The new line was shallow, rarely rising above chest level, but it was a dark night and the enemy were unusually quiet. We delivered our bombs and were instructed to return at 11.00 p.m., which seemed strange and unfair as there were others who could have taken their turn.

When we set off the second time we were unburdened. The significance of this did not strike me at the time. In truth I was too fatigued to think of anything beyond the immediate effort required to move my weary, painful limbs. This time we proceeded above ground, which was more expeditious and less tiring. The night-enfolded battlefield exuded the usual eeriness. There were bobbing lights and an occasional gun flash; now and again a machine-gun stuttered somewhere ahead, but there was little movement and nothing unusual — until we reached the front trench.

The low trench was crammed with men — troops from our D Company and from the 4th Battalion. The parapet was lined with soldiers, their fixed bayonets glinting in the dimly lit night. An attack was being staged. I was struck dumb with amazement. The men were already clambering out of the trench. Hardly had the first man mounted the parapet when the enemy, as though sensing something unusual, sent up a myriad of lights which, bursting overhead, converted night into day. The steel-helmeted figures of the front wave stood out in sharp relief against the unearthly blue illumination. While we hesitated, bewildered by the suddenness of this manoeuvre, an officer pushed his way along the trench threatening with drawn revolver anyone who held back from going over. He pointed it at me. I was flabbergasted. There must be some mistake: we had been told nothing. My astonished terror gave place to anger at the injustice of the whole business. At that moment I would sooner have killed the officer than any German.

To say that I was at the very centre of pandemonium would be to interpret the reality in the mildest way. Only a few moments had elapsed since the first man had mounted the parapet and the night was now throbbing with sound and movement. The heavens were literally opening around us. Tiredness dropped away and my mind became crystal clear. Contemplating the futility of thus attempting a surprise attack upon the enemy I left the trench with the supporting wave. I was still fumbling with my unfixed bayonet as I stumbled into a shell-hole a few paces from the trench. Here I did my best to collect my wits and free the blade from the straps in which my frantic haste had caused it to become entangled. Men were now moving on either side and, with bayonet now fixed, I joined the moving line. We did not get far. Enemy machine-guns were scouring the ground. I slid into a large depression where a number of others were already collected. Hugging the filthy, friendly earth I looked around me, while the stream of bullets passed harmlessly overhead.

I realized that my closest neighbour was dead, but I did not recognize him, for he lay face down in a pool of slimy water. The rifle at his side looked new and almost clean. I yielded to a covetous impulse and exchanged it for mine, which was in a shocking state. The incident shows how, despite intolerable stress, my mind was capable of functioning at an ordinary level of perceptiveness.

The scene was an amazing one. Above the enemy line red, green and yellow lights — signals to the German artillery — rose and fell against the lurid backdrop of gun flashes. It reminded me of those magnificent Brock's benefit nights at the Crystal Palace which I had enjoyed in my youth. But no peacetime pyrotechnic display could have equalled the real thing. The machine-guns traversed back and forth, shearing the ground around us like mighty scythes. Rifles cracked incessantly and bullets spanged into the mud near our heads.

In front we could hear the bursting of hand grenades hurled by the enemy, as much in fright as at specific targets, since there is little evidence that our front wave had got so far. Heavier shells crashed around us, but mainly behind since they were directed against the trench we had left. We were between two fires.

Fortunately I was in a shell-hole that occupied a dip in the ground. It joined a short isolated trench where several other men were collected. An NCO was with us but he was as bewildered as the rest and had nothing to suggest. There was no discernible movement ahead; the first wave had disappeared. Whether any of them survived I cannot say. It seemed highly improbable. There was the impression of a void both in front and behind, no contact with our line. We had to await instructions. Our military training had instilled in us the impossibility of withdrawing without orders. It was an unhappy quandary. There was a good deal of discussion, of criticism, and, as always a variety of suggestions, but no one took control. We had all been rushed too precipitately into the inexplicable situation to be able to cope with it. And so we waited: cold, fearful and wondering.

The flashes faded as the guns stopped firing. The Germans were satisfied that the attack had failed, but they continued to use their machine-guns to good effect. The sky was now filled with stars and the night was bright. Almost any movement could be detected; any attempt to crawl out of our depression was met with a stream of bullets. Thus we lay hour after hour as the night dragged on. I felt myself growing colder and more helpless, as stiff as my dead companion with his head in the mud. What did he look like? Who was he? It did not occur to me to look more closely. I hated the idea of contact. The common practice of rifling the dead of their personal belongings had no attraction for me.

After interminable hours the first grey streaks of approaching dawn appeared in the east and a new terror laid hold of us. If we did not get back before daylight we should be pinned down indefinitely: all day, unable to move, wet through, without food, in front of the enemy's position, a target for any missiles they might choose to hurl at our lines. Anything would be better than that. The danger of our situation galvanized us into action. Across the skyline to our right we saw figures crawling back. We decided to follow their example. 'One at a time,' someone shouted, and the first man made a bolt for our trench. As if a button had been pressed enemy machine-guns opened out, while his lights, so recently quiescent, outshone the pallid dawn. Bullets pelted down and all discretion was cast to the winds. How incredibly fast I moved under the threat of immediate death! I felt the trench literally rushing towards me under the torrent of fire and almost immediately fell on to one of the occupants who swore feelingly at my clumsiness. I gripped the muddy floor with a thankfulness beyond measure. I was back in our front line, safe and unharmed; nothing else mattered.

No official surprise was evinced at our precipitate return. It was assumed that we would stand to with the rest, and this we did as a matter of course. The normal routines proceeded as though nothing had gone amiss.

The enemy did not even bother to indulge in his morning strafe. Full daylight having released us from our watch, I settled myself down almost mechanically in a corner where the trench was deepest. I must have dozed, for when I returned to awareness I heard voices, refined voices, close at hand. A few paces away at the entrance of a primitive shelter — an inflated funk-hole rather than a dug-out — two officers were seated, while an NCO and an orderly were busying themselves nearby. One of the officers was discussing the raid.

It had been hoped to occupy the enemy trench without difficulty, the aim being to straighten out a kink in the line. But it seemed that the coveted trench had been crowded with enemy troops, who may well have had a similar venture in view. In any case their reaction had been instantaneous and our first wave had been blasted in their tracks. An officer was mentioned who had failed to come back. If it were the man with the revolver I felt no compassion for him. It was thought there were many wounded lying between the lines. Their fate was too horrible to contemplate, for neither side was likely to tolerate any movement for fear of a trap.

The officers had rations — bread, biscuits, bully beef and jam — which they shared with men in the vicinity. Never were those unexciting foodstuffs more palatable — manna from heaven in the midst of hell. It was in fact a bright morning and everywhere seemed so quiet that I forgot briefly that I was situated at the very juncture of our world and that of the ruthless enemy who had been threatening all our lives for more than two years. Though I had often in the past imagined such a moment, envisaging it with reverence and awe, this morning the shiver of emotion that shook me had little of the heroic about it.

From the corner where I was sitting the low trench led for a few yards in the direction of the enemy line, then turned sharply to the right beyond my range of vision. Directly ahead I could see in the foreground a narrow fringe of the devastated no-man's-land in which I had spent the night. All was so quiet now: there was no hint of danger. A little later a dramatic incident demonstrated how appearance sadly belied reality. A stooping figure turned the corner, coming in my direction, but he had not stooped low enough. A crisp crack from a sniper's rifle and the soldier lay dead with a bullet through his skull. It happened in a flash. Willing hands pulled the dead man away and warnings about the sniper were passed down the trench.

I sat reflecting on the tragedy enacted so near, so suddenly and in such a matter-of-fact way. It could have been me. Looking back I am surprised I was so little affected. Yet had we not accepted such occurrences as normal incidents of our way of life most of us would probably have lost our reason. As some did, of course. Shortly a second figure appeared, again lulled into a state of false security by the apparent quietness of the scene and a natural disinclination to grovel too closely in the mud. A second victim fell, fortunately this time with only a shoulder wound. He crawled back safely out of sight. During the morning there were many shouts for help and on one occasion a fearless stretcher-bearer disappeared over the back of the trench on an errand of mercy amidst a regular rain of enemy bullets. The majority remained huddled away from harm's reach at the bottom of the shallow trench, praying silently for relief from this precarious situation.

At midday we were ordered back to join our company which had returned to the line we had held during the attack. All was now quiet and I could look about the position without fear. The shattered line had acquired an air of calm since the day before: the dead had gone, the smell of conflict had subsided, memories of more recent agony had already detached my mind from yesterday's torment. In the searching afternoon light I could perceive nothing more than a blasted ditch. Yet I was amazed by the evidence of the mathematical precision of the enemy's bombardment. My own survival seemed an even greater miracle.

During the evening men of the East Yorks came up to relieve us. It was at the time of stand-to and the communication trench was subjected to a mild bombardment. It was as though Fritz was loth to let us go without further toll. At a dangerous spot where the trench flattened out across a sunken road, I saw a number of corpses laid at the side awaiting burial. Their calculated neatness struck a special note of horror within me, while the winking flashes along the horizon warned me that it was too soon to rejoice in this unhallowed land. We came at last to the ridge where we were to leave Pioneer Alley for the open. In front of one of the sandbagged dug-outs each man was served with hot coffee, a draught of thick black liquid that brought a new warmth into my body and made me offer thanks to heaven.

The line moved on, a straggling, weary snake stretching into the gloom, our figures throwing exaggerated shadows from the flares at dug-out openings. Two lone purposeful shells screamed over from the enemy, striking the ground not far from the spot where coffee was being served. After escaping so much, seven more of our company were added to the roll of death and four others were carried away on stretchers; the unkindest blow at the very edge of safety.

Flers Switch was to be our billet for the night. I was too exhausted to look for proper shelter. I sank down on the parapet and was immediately asleep. When I awoke in the morning the ground was mantled with frost, which also covered my great-coat, trousers and puttees, camouflaging me as part of the landscape. I was stiff and cold but such had been my fatigue that I had slept heedlessly through all the rigours of the night and whatever enemy activity there may have been. Our improvised camp was soon astir and the cookers, which had been brought up to meet us, gave glowing promise of breakfast. It was almost good to be alive, but an occasional shell-burst warned us that it was still too soon to bank upon survival. The battalion paraded in motley groups for roll call. There were one hundred and sixty of us present, one company being reduced to fifteen and our C Company being forty strong. Of course there would be many stragglers, as men got mixed up in battles, but there could be no doubt that our casualties had been heavy.

Later in the day we were withdrawn to reserve in Prue Trench, which had been altered out of all recognition since our earlier occupancy. It had been converted by the Royal Engineers into winter quarters with a row of neatly sandbagged dug-outs under semi-circular corrugated iron roofs which, if not exactly shellproof, provided the acme of comfort after our recent exposure.

Unfortunately the cosy atmosphere inside, particularly when we were all tucked up at night, thawed my feet into painful activity. I had been able to forget them during the recent action. Now they became so agonizing that I could bear nothing to touch them. The quietness of our second day in this position was broken by a brief long-distance bombardment, during which a direct hit was registered on one of the dug-outs in the second line, killing three of its occupants and seriously wounding the fourth.

That night it snowed but, packed snugly in our shelter, we kept each other warm, and I should have been content but for my feet. The next day we entrained, a weak and weary collection of human wrecks, at the railhead which had now been brought as far forward as Bazentin-le-Petit. Hereabouts the landscape was acquiring a ship-shape look with new winter quarters springing up like mushrooms in the form of neatly arranged hutments and other amenities. That evening we were back in the old billet under the hanging Virgin in Albert, reclining round a roaring brazier fed by wood which we had scrounged. Here at last, after an interval of twenty-six days, I was able to enjoy a wash and shave. The results were revealing as well as heartening.

Caked with dry mud and scratched unmercifully by every piece of loose wire or barbed stake in the trenches, it is not easy to understand how one's hands and arms had escaped some form of blood poisoning. It should be emphasized that this had been an unusually long period of deprivation, accompanied as it was by a chronic shortage of food and fresh drinking water and not infrequently by periods of soaking rain and slime, an experience exceptional during all my time at the front. Twenty-six days in hell. On my knees I prayed in deep gratitude for my deliverance from that horror, whose forbidding shadows continued to weigh upon all of us, as was too evident from the general conversation.

HISTORICAL NOTE: END OF THE BATTLE OF THE SOMME, 1916

The general Anglo-French attack on 25th September has already been mentioned. By coincidence this was the very day the present writer joined his new regiment in reserve positions behind Mametz Wood. By 3rd October, thrusting towards Bapaume, the village of Eaucourt l'Abbeye had been captured. In the course of this comparatively successful battle 6,000 prisoners were taken by the British alone, and also a number of guns which the enemy was usually able to pull back in these localized operations. A wave of optimism at the evident weakening of enemy resistance was immediately, and literally, dampened by a deterioration of the weather which rendered the ground almost impassable.

Nevertheless, on 7th October Le Sars, on the main Albert-Bapaume road, was stormed, but the ground conditions prevented the taking of the Butte de Warlencourt, an upstanding hillock to the right of the road beyond Le Sars, which the enemy had converted into an almost impregnable strong-point. Assaults on this key-position were to continue with heavy losses during the ensuing weeks, but the Germans were to retain the Butte until the end of the campaign. According to official statements the Butte was never captured, but the author's participation in a stretcher-bearing party from Eaucourt l'Abbeye on 6th November to bring out severely wounded from the front of the Butte indicated that it was then commanded by our troops, perhaps for too short a time for the incident to be officially recorded.

During this phase numerous German counterattacks had been beaten off successfully, except on 23rd October when the enemy recovered important ground in front of Le Sars. During the early part of November, the British gained ground in front of Le Transloy and Grandcourt, but it was all very heavy going. The final battle, from 13th to 18th November took place on the northern sector along the Ancre river which flows through Albert, giving its name to that particular phase of the fighting although the same title, Battle of the Ancre, is officially applied to all these operations from 25th September onwards, to phases of which five different battle names have been given, making it all very confusing. The Battle of the Somme is considered officially to have ended on 19th November, 1916.

The Official History, in the eyes of this one observer at least, gives an accurate if depressing description of both scene and action in these later stages:

> By the middle of October conditions on and behind the battle front were so bad as to make mere existence a severe trial of body and spirit. Little could be seen from the air through the rain and mist, so counterbattery work suffered and it was often impossible to locate with accuracy the new German trenches and shell-hole positions. Objectives could not always be identified from ground level, so that it is no matter for surprise or censure that the British artillery sometimes fired short or placed its barrages too far ahead. The infantry, sometimes wet to the skin and almost exhausted before zero hour, were often condemned to struggle painfully forward through the mud, under heavy fire against objectives vaguely defined and difficult of recognition.[2]

---

[2] Quoted by Lieut-Col. John Baynes in History of the First World War, No. 61 on 'The Somme: The Last Phase', p.1689 (Purnell, 1969-71).

In this terrible First Battle of the Somme[3] British casualties totalled nearly half a million, rather more than the Germans, not surprisingly in view of our predominantly attacking role: 38,000 prisoners were taken, and a thousand square miles of once flourishing countryside was captured, mashed into a shambles that had to be seen and felt and smelt to be believed. Today it will certainly not be believed — apart from the evidence of the numerous carefully planned and tended War Cemeteries and a number of impressive memorials — by those who visit the fair land completely restored under nature's healing hand.

For the combatants it was of course different: only those who died early in the Battle, still expectant of victory could have discerned prospects of victory in the contemporary environment. None who observed the awful morass near the time of curtain fall on November 19th could have had any reason for elation, except in gratitude for personal survival. To adjudge the results of all these sacrifices one would have to await consequences hidden deep in a future that held in store much unanticipated pain and sorrow for all who were then alive.

While the Somme offensive had been proceeding to its slow conclusion in the mud grave and significant events had been taking place on the many home and battle fronts. By a brilliant counter-stroke which recaptured the important key-positions of Fort Vaux and Fort Duaumont, the French had brought to an end the Germans' costly attempt to take Verdun. In the east both the Russians and our recently recruited ally, Rumania, were in dire trouble, while the Germans themselves, surrounded by enemies, were a long way from their high confidence of 1914. Fighting in the mountainous barriers of

---

[3] The Second Battle of the Somme was to take place in 1918.

Northern Italy had produced some territorial gains but at the cost of excessive casualties to both sides. Nowhere in the major European theatres had substantial objectives been achieved.

The world-wide contest had in effect become a war of exhaustion, the outcome of which only time would disclose. To those on all sides who were personally involved, even the General Staffs, 1916 had been a year of frustration and in some quarters, Russia in particular, the original high resolution was beginning to crumble. On all the home fronts, even among the dwindling band of neutrals, pressures were beginning to tell and the toll of human suffering was already incalculable.

Britain in particular, through the unspectacular pressures of the Royal Navy, was tightening the Allies' grip on the Central Powers, while Germany herself with her U-boat offensive was building up to an all-out sea stranglehold on her most dangerous foe. At home, where night-time Zeppelin attacks were giving way to even more frightening day-time aeroplane raids, rationing was further inconveniencing almost everybody. In the autumn a vital change in Government took place: following a Cabinet crisis the Prime Minister, Herbert Henry Asquith (subsequently Earl of Oxford and Asquith), resigned. A classical scholar of quality and statesman of world-wide reputation, he lacked the ruthless drive essential to the successful conduct of a war of the type that had now developed and pressures had built up, particularly as a result of the agonies and apparent failure of the Somme, that rendered a change of leadership essential.

Asquith was replaced by David Lloyd George who despite weighty criticisms was destined to take a dominant part in bringing about the Allies' ultimate victory. He was surely the man of the hour, even as Winston Churchill was to prove to be in the later world conflict.

VII: CASUALTY

It was on 18th November that we arrived back in Albert, where we were to stay till the end of the month, waiting, as it turned out, for the division to be relieved. We spent the days on the usual parades and fatigues, but with little enthusiasm, for recovery from our recent ordeal was to be slow. Everyone was pessimistic about the current operations. There seemed to be little prospect of a decision. Promises of victory, even the capture of Bapaume which was to round off the Somme offensive, had not materialized. At the front were plenty of troops, plenty of guns, plenty of stores: it was like a vast ant-hill and just as inexplicable to the rest of us. With all that fretful movement, accompanied by the noise of the guns, the clanking of transport, the cursing of exasperated mule drivers, and the grumblings of humanity at large, the urge forward seemed frustratingly leisurely and ineffective. We were literally stuck in the mud; the whole army was bogged down.

On the second day I had to report sick with my feet which were very painful. The MO told me to get them rubbed with whale oil and awarded the usual medicine and duty. We were being treated like cattle and I came away feeling like a criminal. Yet others were not so easily rebuffed and many had become daily supplicants. The pain continued: in the day it moderated but at night became hardly bearable. I could not stand anything near my feet. Three days later I could put up with it no longer and, against my better judgment, again reported sick. With no better results, however, and I swore that this should be the last occasion. I noticed for the first time that the skin had broken at the back of the ankle, but it did not look serious.

On our third day the Colonel came to carry out the usual inspection and to deliver a pep talk, of which we took a poor view. He looked well and astonishingly well-groomed, a being from a different universe. We hated his guts. He certainly took no steps to court popularity.

Corry and I were fast becoming close friends. I could not forget the great service he had done me during the attack, when his aid had most certainly preserved my life. I found him a quiet, dry soul, without any of Jimmy's gentleness. He hated soldiering even more than I did, and was not, as far as I could judge, buoyed up by an inner patriotic fire, though to do him justice it may well have existed, for he was not a demonstrative type. Exposure had undermined his health and he had become a regular visitor to the MO.

Despite this new friendship, which was a great consolation, I continued to be haunted by Jimmy's kind face and a heavy feeling of loss which I still failed wholly to believe. As I looked round our bare room, especially in the evenings when the red glow from the brazier threw weird shadows across the equipment-encumbered walls and silhouetted the haggard faces of my companions, I wondered sometimes if I were still alive or already dead and in some special sort of limbo. All sense of space and time had gone and the world of trees and sunshine appeared as mythical as the faces of loved ones which the passage of a few brief months had almost erased from my memory. A few months, centuries rather, time interminable in unimaginable hell. Someone laughs. I clutch my leg and the pressure brings back a sense of reality. The dream has passed and like a child I feel an overwhelming desire to cry, a desire that can be satisfied, silently, only in the depth of night.

In the evenings some went out in search of relaxation, possibly in one of the few *estaminets* that still survived, with great profit to their owners, where drink and other cheer might be obtained. Cinema shows were being organized every evening. Although I had been an addict of the new moving pictures from boyhood days and especially of Charlie Chaplin, who was a particular favourite of the Forces, I did not make the effort required to walk the distance of a few streets, so painful were my feet. I am sure I was also influenced by the thought of being caught in one of those desultory evening strafes, which on one occasion during our stay caused the audience to leave in a hurry. In any case there were letters to write, the few papers that got through the postal complex to read, the warming brazier to look into, and at all times a serious 'chat' hunt in one's shirt to undertake. The trouble was that our shirt seams were regularly choked with eggs so that the incineration of bloated adults in the candle flame — a popular method — only hastened the birth of a new and even more ravenous generation of lice. The itching recommenced very soon after the shirt had been 'purified', leaving one with only the consolation, for what it was worth, of having had a murderous revenge upon some of one's tormentors.

Another effort was officially launched to fill in some of the gaps among the specialists. This time I was assigned to a course of instruction under the Signalling Officer in a neighbouring billet. This was not only interesting but suited me well because of the state of my feet, but again it quickly petered out and we were despatched on working parties. In the morning we went out at 6.30 a.m. when it was still pitch, to dig a drainage trench a mile or so out of town in the coldest and dreariest weather. As it happened we were operating near the site of a recently occupied Canadian encampment which had been abandoned for proper winter quarters. The shelters had been ingeniously constructed from wooden ammunition boxes which were easily dismantled. Each man extracted a box for firewood and the returning column in the afternoon must have presented a comical appearance. The boxes were so beautifully morticed and finished that it seemed a shame to burn them, though they did make excellent fuel, then getting very short, and there was no alternative use for them. That was another incident in war's tale of colossal waste.

On other days we were employed as scavengers in the streets of Albert. Armed with brooms and scrapers we sallied forth to wade in the liquid mud and push it ineffectively this way and that. The weather continued very cold and the freezing water brought back acute pain in my feet. Once when we got back to billet after one of these expeditions some of us found our names 'on the peg' for leaving dusty rifles hanging on the walls.

The good news came on 30th November that we were to be moved back, and the thought of again seeing the untouched countryside, even at that time of year, heartened me, for these were few trees in shattered Albert. The following day we marched back to Bresle, a small village just off the Albert-Amiens road. I did my best to keep going but the effort proved too much for my strength. After a halt the road came up to meet me and, for the first and last occasion during my army career, I fell out of a marching column and was brought in on a passing G.S. wagon. I felt disgraced.

Thus I was bound to report sick the following morning, despite my previous resolution. Now I was given 'light duty' which entailed mess-orderly fatigues at the cook house. Little else was possible, for I was now hobbling about like an old man.

Bresle was a pleasant little place, although our billets left much to be desired. The divisional canteen occupied a large barn in the village and was promisingly stocked for such time as we should receive our next pay, now long overdue. In the evening the divisional band gave a cheerful concert, mainly of selections from musical comedies which were enthusiastically applauded by a large audience. I was surprised to discover that we had such a good band and felt more content than I had done for a very long time.

This feeling lasted well into the following day, which was 3rd December. After a very welcome visit to the brigade baths and still being on light duty, I was able to pass the time quietly in the billet while the company was on parade. I paid a visit to the little shop opposite, but by this time funds had run low. In the courtyard our newly-appointed sanitary men with yellow armlets were busily getting the incinerator working; everywhere there was a general sense of briskness, which was a change from previous experience. Occasionally the Orderly Corporal came through the billet and chatted in a friendly way. I was beginning to find the northerners much more approachable. They were certainly rough and difficult to know. Our shared adventures had no doubt made a difference, so many of the older hands having gone. That morning, at any rate, I felt that things could have been much worse and that if only my feet would mend there would be little to grumble about. Then I received a shock. The Orderly Sergeant ordered me to prepare to join a working party due to leave immediately. Dismayed by this threat to my recently-acquired peace of mind I protested that I was receiving medical attention and therefore unfit to undertake special work. He told me that the battalion was going into training and it would be in my own interest to be away. I did not believe him, for the clear truth was that I would be a nuisance and this was his smart way of solving a difficulty.

Thus it was that at 1.40 p.m., after bidding Corry and others goodbye with much regret, I joined the waiting party. There were twenty men in the charge of an officer who appeared as confused as the rest of us. It was expected that the march would be short; indeed transport was vaguely hinted at. At every turn of the road, which wound forward through pleasantly rural countryside, we anticipated our destination and were a dozen times disappointed. The officer was clearly feeling his way. Now and again he halted and considered, made a turn to right or left — and so we meandered on. After a few paces I felt my feet becoming chafed and the pain returning. My pack was barely supportable in the circumstances and frequently I had to grit my teeth to avoid repeating my previous escapade, a possibility I hated to contemplate. Only hope kept me going during those early stages.

After a time the pain went and I shuffled along, automatically, as in a dream. The little country cottages became unreal, a flattened pattern against a background of fantastic shapes. The road twisted and turned, we cursed and blasphemed and thus relieved our tensions. We rested often and every fresh start was a worse wrench than the previous one. Late in the afternoon we entered the village of Freshencourt, and fell out by the roadside. Tea was served. Similar parties from the Durham and Yorkshire regiments joined us, proving that the whole operation had been carefully planned, despite the officer's assumed innocence. I had my pack carried when we resumed the march, but conditions got worse and worse. The line lengthened, straggled badly and halts became more frequent. The majority of us limped along like old men. But I managed not to fall out. At last at 9.30 p.m. we reached Allonville where we were billeted in a barn.

The following morning found us in a pleasant wood about two miles away on the Amiens road making fascines which the R.E. used for constructing temporary roads, usually across soggy ground. We worked with billhook and axe, collecting suitable long branches which were bound into long straight bundles with wire. The work was healthy but extremely boring. A welcome meal was served on our return to billets. After the third day the NCO, who had no doubt observed my painful struggling, instructed me to report sick. As it happened the 39th Casualty Clearing Station was situated in the village. The doctor shook his head with sympathy and said nothing could be done. I should just have to rest. With this rather ineffective diagnosis I returned to the billet and set about treating my chafes with the boracic powder which the medical people had supplied. My feet now looked bad enough but the pain had gone, and I felt much better in myself.

I could do nothing now but rest in the billet, passing the time with whatever reading matter I could lay my hands on. It was not easy to move about even to meet the needs of nature. I had to make my way to the public army latrine which was set up just off the village street. One day I remember well being accosted sympathetically by an Australian traffic policeman who had a cushy job there and made no attempt to hide his appreciation of his good fortune. He told me that he was a policeman at home in civil life and spoke in an awed voice about the horrors of the battle area, which he obviously hoped would never be his lot.

Naturally I looked forward each day to the return of the working party, when there would be a good hot meal and pleasant chatter. Not that the men were very pleased with the position. We were isolated, many had been parted from their closest friends and, worst of all, we were very short of money, if we had any at all. Representations about this were made to the officer, but he was in a similar position and found contact with the battalion difficult.

On the evening of the ninth day it was decided to move us to different billets in St Gratien. I was carried by the transport, but on our arrival we had to wade across a courtyard swimming in liquid mud and my feet suffered further damage.

I continued to rest and to become more and more depressed. I no longer had the feeling that the dressing station was handy in case of emergency, nor was there prospect of treatment for my feet which were obviously not healing. Others were beginning to fall sick, so that I was rarely alone in the billet and in that respect the position was brighter. In addition, a young fellow from one of the other companies had constituted himself a sort of protector and aide, to fetch my meals and do other services after his return from working party. His kindness was boundless and I must sometimes have appeared an ungrateful hound in my unwarranted touchiness. How strange we humans are! My companion-in-arms who was so kind to me left with me no impress of his personality, yet over half a century later I still remember his considerate deeds.

The whole group was becoming increasingly discouraged and hating the prospect of having to spend Christmas away from the unit and the normal Christmas celebrations; and we were still without pay. Yet they kept bright and in the evenings when the brazier was alight there was invariably a sing-song and the retailing of yarns. Nothing had happened by 21st December and we were reconciled to spending Christmas where we were. The officers had promised to do their best. Christmas mail had begun to arrive including some parcels, and great was the rejoicing in the share-out. I had received one and others were promised.

By the time the working party returned next day there was a noticeable atmosphere of change. A death had occurred in a neighbouring billet and as usual the official wires began to hum. As a preliminary our officer came round to inspect his sick cases. He looked at me doubtfully and wanted to know what I had been doing all this time. In his voice and expression I detected a tentative accusation of malingering. I pulled off the grubby bandages. His voice changed immediately. 'He must go away at once, Corporal,' he said hurriedly, and passed on to our other casualty. His compassion was worse than his accusation. To send me away at this very juncture seemed merely a way of depriving me of my parcels. Besides I had no wish to leave my colleagues in adversity. But there was no time to think or protest. For once the haste was unseemly. Willing hands helped me to adjust my equipment. An exchange of 'so longs' and I was carried by a number of my companions to a waiting G.S. wagon. The Corporal called laughingly for early news of Blighty and in a turmoil I was conveyed once again to the 39th Casualty Clearing Station.

I was admitted without question, seeming to receive V.I.P. treatment, and immediately found myself alone in a double-walled tent with yellow canvas frieze and hangings. All my kit was taken away, except the haversack that held my personal belongings. I was hustled into a hot bath and handed clean underclothing. My feet were dressed and swathed in bandages of a dazzling whiteness. I was given an anti-tetanus injection by the doctor and then tucked into a proper bed with white sheets and pillows. Such a transformation there never was. I wanted to laugh, only because it would have been absurd to cry. And so I lay there expecting at any moment to wake from my wonderful dream.

The following morning I was moved into a further tent and there quickly visited by a doctor who, I was sure, would order me straightway to get up and go about my business. Having no pain now I could not convince myself that my illness was anything but a sham, a shocking subterfuge aiming at the evasion of my responsibilities. I knew nothing about psycho-analysis, otherwise I might have discovered a more erudite interpretation of my feelings. The doctor came to no brusque decision but was in fact very kind, as was everybody. I could no longer be in the army! I asked the orderly, diffidently, whether I should be staying long, and was surprised when he replied that I should not. Later he came back and told me I should be moved further down no one was kept long there. I was sceptical, imagining that was his idea of a joke. The food was good and well cooked, everywhere was spotless. All I wanted to do was to lie and daydream. Only one thing worried me: there was a rain stain on one of the yellow canvas panels at the opposite side of the tent....

The following morning — Christmas Eve — I was awakened soon after daybreak for ablutions and a basin of tea, in accordance with hospital ritual, and dozed until breakfast time. Preparations were immediately put in hand for my removal and I discovered that the orderly had not been joking. Packed on my stretcher into a motor ambulance in company with three other cases we were soon speeding towards Corbie railway station. The motor travelled swiftly along winding country lanes, jolting over every pot-hole. Through the flaps at the back I caught an occasional glimpse of the landscape in all its heavenly peacefulness. My companions were badly wounded cases and the constant vibration forced groans of pain from their lips. I could imagine how they felt and realized I had much to be thankful for. The Red Cross train which awaited us was comfortably appointed and I was soon pleasingly settled in one of the upper cots. The orderlies could hardly have been more attentive. Their job must have irked them at times. Of course it was comfortable and comparatively safe but some of their tasks were not pleasant and they had to witness the most heartrending sights. One had to be cut out for that sort of thing and I knew that it would not have been for me. Surrounded by all the evidence of the season of good will I could not banish thoughts of the battle that went on unceasingly up yonder and of all the mud and muddle that Christmas could do nothing to alleviate. We were fed and given magazines to read. To me the journey was a delight. But there were many who could find little cheer in the trip. However steadily the train travelled, it could not fail to torment their wounded bodies. Some had to have their dressings adjusted. Only once did I see an orderly out of humour with a patient — a man opposite who kept up a continual grouse. Needless to say he was not badly hurt.

Besides the stretcher cases there were a number of walking wounded who were consistently cheerful. They told stories, cracked jokes and, above all, discussed with concentrated interest the prospects of early peace, in which, I noticed, the orderlies had more faith than we had. It was not until 2.00 a.m. on the following morning that the train drew into Rouen, where, in front of the medical huts, we were sorted out in the artificial light by the RAMC men, but not without difficulty. My label, marked with the somewhat cryptic description 'I.C.T. Feet', was checked in due course and I was bundled off by ambulance to the No.6 General Hospital in the town.

In the early hours the ward, already decorated for the festive season, presented a sight weird but full of promise. The night nurse whispered words of welcome and pushed a screen round my bed. She was the first Englishwoman I had spoken to since coming over. The dream now, I felt, was becoming preposterous. Then a bath of water was brought and I was told to wash myself all over before getting to bed. This at the time seemed slightly unreasonable; but dreams always are unreasonable, so I did what I was told, watching fearfully in the dim light of the ward lest the nurse should trespass beyond the edge of the screen.

Then, spotlessly clean and free from lice, I crawled into my new and even more sumptuous bed and but a few moments later, as it seemed, opened my eyes on a scene of Christmas gaiety. A Merry Christmas, indeed. Never had the words a truer ring. Holly and mistletoe and paper decorations were strung gaily across the ward. 'A Merry Christmas.' Words of welcome and good cheer passed from bed to bed. We were not strangers.

After breakfast the beds were remade and the ward tidied in readiness for the doctor's visit. The Sister looked at my feet and said it was only a question of time. One thing I noticed at once, an absence that had the impact of a shock: there was no bad language here and I trembled lest I should forget myself and die of shame.

The doctor arrived with due ceremony, and the nurses and convalescent men in their blue uniforms came to attention. This was the most important moment of the day. I was the second bed on the left-hand side of the door. He knew the man in the first bed well, a serious case of an arm smashed by an explosive bullet, and one of special interest to the medical an. A brief conversation and the doctor approached my bed. I felt nervous. Judgment was about to be pronounced — and the whole ward watched with concern. Under the gaze of the doctor, Sister and nurses I felt like an impostor and wondered what sort of punishment I deserved. My feet came under the professional eye; the Sister murmured something in a low voice and handed the doctor the chart board from the wall at the head of the bed. He scrawled something very much like a 'B' across the corner of the chart and passed on to the next bed. Its occupant was very ill — a bad case of trench fever. After a brief but obviously serious conversation with the Sister, the doctor took the man's chart board and again scrawled an unmistakeable 'B'.

My heart was beating fast. Did this mean...? A stranger in blue strolled up and commented, 'You're both going to Blighty'. An impossible joy took possession of me. This was how it must feel to be reprieved. What a Christmas present! There were no words to describe such an emotion. I wanted to shout, to laugh, to sing. Instead I closed my eyes and laid back in an ecstasy that knew no bounds. At that moment I remembered the sergeant who had acted so unkindly in placing me on working party, and realized that due to his action my disability had become so aggravated as to send me home.

As soon as the doctor had left the ward, discipline relaxed and the four or five Blighty cases were overwhelmed with congratulations. None were kinder than those less fortunate. It was a jolly day with the distribution of many small personal gifts from well-wishers at home and a traditional Christmas dinner of turkey and plum pudding. During the evening there was a concert for the nurses and walking cases. The trench fever case had been taken away during the afternoon to join the boat convoy which carried the worst cases down river to Le Havre.

We left the following morning in an ordinary train for the seaport and the short journey took most of the day. The discomfort we did not mind in view of our destination, but the lack of food was less acceptable after yesterday's plenty. Our real disappointment came, however, when, after our arrival at 7.00 p.m., we learned that the boat would not cross that night. Our stretchers were arranged in a temporary hospital on the quay. It was only a short delay yet disappointment was universal: nothing could satisfy us until we reached the other side. The stretcher next to mine was occupied by a jolly red-faced man from the West Country. We were soon exchanging reminiscences about the front and I was glad of this distraction from the rather dreary hut and the murmur of the waves outside. He looked so fit that I wondered what he was doing on a stretcher. Then he told me that he had been a postman in civil life and had led a healthy existence in Devonshire. In France he had had the good fortune to be attached as medical orderly to a doctor who had taken an interest in him. The hard life overseas had undermined his health and the early stages of consumption were suspected, a common and fatal disease in those days. In the normal course it was unlikely that he would have been sent home in time; I hope it was in time and that he was soon pacing his Devonshire lanes again. He was a wonderfully cheery fellow.

Next day we were taken aboard the hospital ship *Glenart Castle*, later to become a casualty of the enemy's submarine campaign. I did not like being taken below, but there was nothing to be done about that. We were arranged in two tiers in cots suspended to minimise the ship's vibration. Wounds were dressed and everything was done to make us comfortable. We did not leave till 8.00 p.m. and happily the sea was so smooth that, but for the muffled throb of the engines, it would have been difficult to know we were moving. The cot adjacent to mine was occupied by a stalwart Guardsman, also a trench foot case, whose feet were still in the painful stage. He groaned most of the time. His feet were uncovered and had a ghastly pallor. He was not the sort of man to be easily affected by pain and my pity for him was tempered by an idea that I may have been too self-critical of my own reactions to the early stages of this dismal complaint.

Several Red Cross trains were drawn up at the siding in Southampton when we arrived in the morning. We were asked to designate the part of the country we should prefer for being in hospital. Naturally I chose London, which was no doubt overcalled for eventually I found myself on the train bound for the West Country. Everything on the platform looked spick and span and cheerfully English. The paper-stall and its attendant were to me the most attractive, and at the same time least believable, part of the picture. At Cardiff we were carried to waiting ambulances by kindly spare-time volunteers, men above military age who, despite their uniforms, remained civilians. Thus, on 28th December, I arrived at the 3rd Western General Hospital in Howard Gardens, Cardiff and was soon made comfortable.

It was a wonderful feeling to be back in the old country with the love that only the returned exile can have in his heart, with the sea between oneself and the unforgettable horror. Yet that was already sinking into the background of my consciousness, its stark outlines blurred by a sense of unreality. Was it to be wondered therefore that people at home had scant appreciation of what it was like over there?

I was in a small square ward with two beds against each wall. The nurses were kind but businesslike, the male orderlies cheery and hard-working: mopping, slopping, scrubbing, moving screens, coming and going at all times with bottles and bedpans, theirs was not a task to be envied. The food was to prove ample and well-cooked. The early morning washing routine, a basic hospital rule, was heartily disliked by all. We had a gramophone with a tin horn, which we thought so good then, and would find it painful to listen to now, and a plentiful supply of books, which were untold wealth to me. Stacked on the table by my bed was a pile of novels, well-thumbed books, stories of all kinds. I had already sorted them over many times without being able to decide where to make a start. Anyway it was pleasant just to lie back and listen to the others talking.

The ward was about equally divided between surgical and trench foot cases. The latter was prevalent at that period, no doubt largely on account of conditions on the Somme, but after this the disease dwindled rapidly as the authorities began to ensure proper preventive measures. One young fellow, recovering from a number of wounds, was greatly envied on account of his large visiting list. The arrival of a visitor was always a great event in the ward.

In a bed on the other side of the room an artillery driver was slowly recovering from fractured legs. He was forced to lie on his back with a large wicker frame over his limbs, a tiresome position which he bore with fortitude and good humour though he used the bluest of language, except when nurses were present. Not that this would have affected them much after all they had heard and experienced. A Scots infantry sergeant with serious head wounds occupied the bed next to mine. Shrapnel had narrowly missed his brain and he had a gold plate above the forehead. One night I woke up suddenly to discover the night nurse sitting on his bed, confirming my earlier rather vague suspicions. I discretely snored myself off to sleep again, which was not too difficult. It was he who solved my reading problem by advising me to read Gene Stratton Porter whose Limberlost tales were popular at that time. I started with *Freckles* but while I found the rural setting delightful I could not get over my surprise at the sergeant's choice. I would have expected William le Queux or Fergus Hume to be more in his line.

My feet were healing gradually with the rest and constant applications of boracic powder. It was clear that the medical people were unsure how to treat trench feet. I heard grim stories of the loss of toes and even of the amputation of feet which had turned blue and were rotting. I counted myself fortunate to get off so lightly. One day, with a view to restoring circulation, the application of lemon juice was tried on all cases of trench feet in the ward. The resulting antics were so funny that the ward was convulsed with laughter, but the remedy was not repeated so presumably was not considered of much use. Probably in my case good circulation had made a lot of difference.

By 1st January 1917 we were all full of our own ideas about the war and hopes for an early conclusion, though optimism was far from universal. The artillery driver believed we should lose, after 'they' had mucked everything up. The sergeant, almost as pessimistic, did think that eventually we should win but only after many years of fighting. He went on to assert that he was not really interested since he was now out of it. Before the end of the week I had begun to hobble about with a stick and on 8th January I was marked for convalescence and transferred to the Red Cross Hospital at Bridgend. This establishment had been set up in a large private house known as 'Cartrefle', situated on the outskirts of the town. The nurses were mainly volunteers from among the ladies of the neighbourhood and like their more professional Matron they were kindness itself. In our room were four other patients besides myself: two hefty Guardsmen with leg wounds, a young infantryman recovering from a stomach wound and an elderly fellow who had been operated on for piles, a rather messy business in those days. Fortunately we all got on very well together. Our daily task was to make the beds and polish the floors, which shone with a high glaze resulting from many a hundred such polishings. We could go out unaccompanied for two hours morning and afternoon, but severe weather prevented full enjoyment of the concession. Our days were passed, pleasurably enough, in playing cards, listening to the wheezy gramophone, telling scandalous tales and reading.

The first time I went out wearing the bright blue uniform with regulation red tie I felt conspicuous and nervous, but soon got accustomed to it. The townsfolk were considerate and went out of their way to make themselves known and to arrange numerous socials and other entertainments. Altogether we were thoroughly spoiled. On two evenings a week we were taken by the Sister officially to the pictures. In our group was a young American who had enlisted in the British Army and claimed to have been present at Mons, though it is difficult to see how this could have been. He was a wonderful hand at telling the tale and, while we appreciated his cooperation, his colossal cheek and self-assurance reduced his popularity.

The impact of the war on the general standards of morality was evident in Bridgend as everywhere else. Or was it that the war brought to the surface what was always latent and presented less restricted opportunities than was the case under peacetime conditions? To hear the men in the hospital talk one could have been excused for concluding that there was not a moral woman in the town. It was unkind of us to malign the people who were so kind to us, yet it had to be admitted that a substantial percentage of the stories contained an element of truth. One could not deny the evidence of ones eyes. There were among us men who heartily disliked lewdness, but public opinion caused one to hide one's prudery. A tale was told and the roar of laughter placed the seal on the listeners' appreciation. No one wished to be singled out as a straight-laced fool or an artful rogue.

Social occasions were varied enough. Sometimes there was a whist drive — not very exciting for the devotees of pontoon and brag — and usually an organized entertainment of some sort. One of the most terrifying was when we were invited to tea by the Young Women's Christian Association and were outnumbered by four to one. Even the practised lady-killers were subdued on that occasion. At one of these affairs a comic turn was given by a sergeant from the front who was the living image of Bairnsfather's 'Old Bill'. He told us that he had known Captain Bairnsfather and, whether this was true or not, his bushy moustache and twinkling smile made him the prototype of the famous cartoon character. He was indeed a comedian and kept the audience in fits of laughter. His mission, we learned, was the arrest of a deserter: such a merry escort was truly incongruous.

One afternoon a party of us was selected for a special visit to the stately home of a Colonel Nichols, one of the local gentry, whose daughter, Commandant of the hospital, we often saw in her neat blue uniform with gold officer's star. As the car drove past the lodge gates and along the drive we could glimpse through the trees the frontage of a big Georgian-style house. We were ushered into a large hall, each man striving in his own way to stifle his nervousness, and it was immediately evident that the interior of the building was not to belie its outward promise. Here in fact was an authentic version of the impressive country mansion so often conjured up in novel and history book, and since those days, with the transformation of our society, thrown open to be viewed by all and sundry.

We were received by the Colonel's wife and his two charming daughters, who at once put us at ease, though I strongly felt that the crowd of blue-garbed Tommies looked completely out of place in the quiet austerity of that impressive hall. The conversation soon became general, but most of it went over my head, for I could not tear my eyes away from the collection of leather-bound tomes ranged on shelves covering the walls from floor to ceiling — untold wealth to me.

Soon came tea in the long dining room, and a new onset of nervousness when I found myself seated at the right hand of the Colonel, who had just made his appearance and introduced himself. I need not have been apprehensive, for some of the others had already visited the hall and no undue demands in the form of conversation were made on me. We were indeed made to feel at home, but I considered it the greatest good fortune to have survived without upsetting my cup.

After tea we were ushered into the Colonel's study, where we were shown and discussed numerous recently published magazines and books which had not yet graduated to library status. I remember that among these were a number of Bairnsfather cartoons, on which the Colonel was evidently keen to obtain our candid comments. We assured him that they accurately interpreted important aspects of our lives at the front.

This was not the end of the business, for three weeks later I had a real shock when the Sister told me that I had been chosen, together with Billings, a postman in civil life, to repeat the visit on our own. I could not understand the reason for this distinction, except that we were both servants of the Post Office. My first reaction was to impress the Sister with the idea that I was feeling too off colour to do justice to such an occasion, but she had no intention of substituting someone else, and we were duly collected in state by the car. The entertainment went very much as before, except that we now received individual attention and I had not the support of the crowd. The two girls, lovely themselves, took us out on the beautiful terrace overlooking gardens which in a month or two would burst into a riot of colour. After tea the Colonel in his study went out of his way to question us on our respective occupations with evident interest. I was glad that my companion was by nature extremely voluble, and covered himself with glory. It should be emphasized that, in those days when class divisions were still clearly defined, there was absolutely no suspicion of condescension on the part of our hosts. During that war, whatever we may have thought of ourselves, the men in uniform, and particularly the hospital convalescents, were esteemed as heroes, and this applied to the entire Bridgend community.

As the weeks of convalescence passed, I learned to walk without a stick and felt thoroughly fit. Discussions about women and war alternated with grouses about the food — dislike of curry on Wednesdays. We got fed up and wanted to go home, even though that meant leaving our haven of rest. During February better news had been coming in from France, where the Germans were withdrawing to massively prepared positions at the Hindenburg Line which, with all their hard-earned experience of trench warfare, they had designed to be impregnable. The newspapers, as usual, were jubilantly claiming the withdrawal as a victory, and no doubt to the troops in France as well as to us at home this considerable advance across country and through towns scarcely touched by war was a strange and extremely heartening occurrence. The changed circumstances at the front could, without a real grasp of the strategic implications of the advance, be represented as the just fruits of the awful Somme offensive which, with Bapaume at last safely behind our line, seemed now to have been justified. Hopes of an early victory were again in the ascendant and the attractions of convalescence proportionately diminished. After all, the majority of us were far from home in South Wales and yearning to see our families again.

Even the counter-pull during these last few weeks of a touch of personal romance was not sufficient to deflect my longing. At one of our socials I had been introduced to Gwladys, elder daughter of Lewis the well-established baker in the High Street. She was charming and attractive and I was extremely flattered by the fact that she had earned from my colleagues the genuine, if somewhat facetious, title 'Belle of the Ball'. After the first tongue-tied exchanges I felt my normal shyness dissolving under her charm and discerned in her response a natural liking that could not fail to thrill me. We became immediate friends and she always sought me out at subsequent entertainments. But I was still the romantic boy under the magic spell of a suppressed love for a school-chum's sister whom I had known and admired from a distance for many years.

During the remaining days at the hospital we found reason for dissatisfaction at the way we were treated. Beds were emptying quickly, most of the cases leaving at approximately the same time, and no new patients were arriving. By 20th February there were few of us left, too few to attend the social arranged for that evening. Notice of our departure on the following morning was held up until the last moment — by design we thought and had good reason to believe that the warrants could have been made out for a day earlier in accordance with previous departures. The ten days leave to which we were officially entitled was far too short to brook curtailment by even a few hours.

The delay in announcing our imminent departure made it possible to arrange only to see my dear friend at the door of her father's shop on our way to the station in the morning. My heart sank when she was not there and I realized that I should not see her again. What went wrong I had no idea, and was too tied by my routine and fearful of jeopardizing my leave to take any initiative at the time. It was one of those missed occasions that could have made all the difference to my life. As it was Gwladys and I remained pen-friends until the end of the war.

So in the morning of 21st February 1917, I left Bridgend with my longing for home tempered by a heavy heart. I had enjoyed quiet happy days in a friendly environment that was paradise compared with what had gone before.

VIII: RECUPERATION

Who could have resisted the lure of the hero-worship with which all returning warriors were welcomed, the bitter-sweet meetings which were at the same time farewells and the tranquil evenings by the family hearth which made unreal the events of the past? The days of leave were as fleeting as a dream. Shadowing the profound joy was the bewildering truth that what we had experienced was entirely outside the comprehension of the sheltered folks at home.

There was also the tenuous vision of love which my immaturity failed to will to life, denying the passionate present for some impossible fantasy of the future. Even when one evening I took Grace to see a popular spy drama at the Lyceum Theatre, my lips failed to utter the words my heart had murmured in every dark moment of hell. This callow lover's dream would not be worth mentioning were it not for its tremendous influence upon my morale during those days of horror that had passed and were still to come. Added to my burning conviction of the justice of our cause, my constant communications with the dear ones at home, the inspiration I derived from the well-thumbed *New Testament* which I carried in my tunic, this romantic dreaming completed the spiritual armour which enabled me to survive the battle unscathed. Yet the girl I worshipped was never to know how deeply and how long I had loved her.

Nor was I to meet during that leave, or ever again, her brother and my closest friend, Eddie Collins, who had eagerly enlisted early in 1915, giving a false age as had so many others, but was still in training as a heavy gunner when my more reluctant self had already graduated under fire. He had earned the approbation of his officers, and was now a bombardier about to go with his battery overseas.

All too soon, on a drab day early in March, I found myself forlorn and in company equally glum, on the train from Kings Cross to the north. We were bound for Catterick, the bleak Yorkshire depot of the Northumberland Fusiliers. If there could have been a more gloomy place in these islands, at that time of year with snow on the ground, it would have been difficult to imagine. The strict routine did nothing to ameliorate the conditions, and was not intended to do so. The personnel of the camp was divided into two distinct groups: on the one hand the permanents on the staff, instructors and base details of all sorts, some of whom had been across the seas and others who had managed to find soft jobs without having taken any sort of risk, but all at one in their scheming to avoid being sent to the battlefield: on the other hand we, the convalescents, who were to be prepared as quickly as possible for another dose of active war. We all knew where we stood and there was no love lost between the two groups.

Our depot battalion was under the command of a Colonel who showed little liking for his troops and whose antipathy was returned with interest. The permanents feared him, for he held their lives in his hands; the convalescents hated him, for we had no use for the parade-ground soldier. He was indeed a great parade-ground soldier, a peacetime territorial too old for active service who never missed an opportunity to have the eight companies of the depot battalion drawn up in full parade for general salute, with band playing and every buckle and button polished to catch the least gleam of sun through rain-laden clouds. Nor did he hesitate to bawl at his officers and order drill to be done again should there be the slightest hitch.

When we returned from route march, or left church parade on Sundays, the whole assembly had to march in column of fours past his burly figure on horse-back, shouting 'Look at me' at the least flicker of a man's eye-lid; a command that provoked, in stage whispers which he may well have heard, 'We don't want ter look at yer, yer ugly bastard!'

Only on Fridays when he visited the mess hut at the midday meal did we feel that he might sometimes be on our side. There was not a lot to grumble at on ordinary days, but on Fridays we enjoyed an excess of food and special attention was evidently given to the cooking. He put the fear of God into all the base details. We wondered what happened to the excess on the other days and what would have been disclosed had the Colonel surprised the cooks by changing his inspection day. Such a possibility was not provided for in the rule books!

Nothing was omitted to make our lives at the depot as miserable as possible. The army's capacity to harass us was pushed to the limits, so that only the permanent staff wanted to stay at Catterick. Probably that was part of the grand design, to do everything possible to make us want to return to hell. And so, when one day a rumour spread that tropical kit had been seen arriving at the quartermaster's store, some of us took the active step of volunteering for Mesopotamia, where we believed the regiment had a detachment. Not that we had any illusions that the Middle East would be a home from home. Its particular discomforts had been sufficiently reported in the press, but to us its ills would be different from those we had endured in France, and we preferred a different devil if there had to be a second occasion. In any case the Sergeant-Major evinced no enthusiasm when a group of us intimated our preference to him at the Orderly Room. He merely put this down as another effort at 'dodging the column', an activity which much of his effort at the camp was devoted to frustrating.

I was pleased to run into Corry at the camp. He too had been invalided home at Christmas. Unfortunately we were destined to see little of each other for an outbreak of measles led to the segregation of his hut for some time. There was quite an epidemic in progress. Scabies also was prevalent and numerous inspections were undertaken by the Medical Officer, as a result of which many a soldier with a suspicious rash was mysteriously wafted away with all his kit. Although I suffered from a rash across my chest no medical man ever took the slightest interest in it.

I soon settled down to the routine of the camp and found the atmosphere of the large hut friendly enough, for were we not all companions in adversity, at one in our intention to dodge as many fatigues as possible? These were frequent and often futile, such as going about the camp in large groups to pick up non-existent paper. At any moment we could be fallen in for some inspection — perhaps of our boots. I remember that at the first pay parade, at which I received five shillings in return for a smart salute made under the eyes of the watching platoon, I was ordered curtly to get my hair cut.

It was dangerous to hang about the huts after parade. Orderly corporals and sergeants were constantly on the prowl for victims to put on fatigue, possibly to fill a gap on one of the patrols that walked the main road into Richmond, scrutinizing soldiers on pleasure bent to ensure that they were properly dressed: belts done up and correctly adjusted, buttons buttoned, and so forth. That was a hateful duty, for during the evening the members of the patrol were subjected to many baleful glances. The inspectors were much inspected.

The YMCA and Church Army huts in the camp were comfortably equipped and well supported, but unfortunately they had to be placed out of bounds because of the measles epidemic. On many days the inherent drabness of the place was masked by heavy snowfalls — which afforded the authorities further scope to add to our spare-time labours.

At last spring did make a tentative appearance, very wanly, I thought, on those northern moors when compared with our kindlier southern countryside. In the lightening evenings I went for walks, sometimes with a companion, but frequently alone, for although not at that time much of an intellectual I found the normal conversation of my camp-mates rather banal. At first I found the countryside depressing and Richmond, except for its fine castle, a drab little place. The streets of the town were usually thronged with square-pushing Tommies and with young girls in twos and threes, arm in arm and smirking at every passing male who showed the least interest. This was the Monkey Parade, as it came to be known, typical of all towns in the neighbourhood of camps and regarded as customary in the 'twenties when youngsters had little else than the pictures to occupy their spare time and insufficient money for many such visits. Neither this square-pushing nor drinking in pubs had much attraction for me, so I was a poor companion to most of my camp colleagues.

With the real onset of spring, I began to feel a special sympathy for the Yorkshire scene and to plan longer walks through those many villages with an old-world air and fascinating names — Bampton-on-Swale, Hauxwell, Hunton — each with its own rural charm to temper the bleakness of the general landscape.

Unceasingly the scheme of training went forward, its object being to make us fit to fight again; and with most of us it was successful. We were taken out on short route marches, and my distinct limp gradually disappeared. We were given almost continuous arms drill outside, and lectures indoors when the weather rendered such exercises impossible. Yet we were not as we had been before. No longer were we overawed by the instructors' tales about gas or greatly impressed by news of the latest gadgets at the front. The prestige of the unknown no longer influenced us. We had become sceptics, remembering the mud and the incompetence that had characterized our active service.

There were, however, the special occasions. On the night of 24th March there was much blowing of bugles and we were ordered to stand to and confined to camp. Rumour was divided between an expected German attack on the East Coast, more trouble in Ireland and a break-through in France. During the following afternoon there was a general inspection and on the third day the scare, such as it was, seemed to be over. A few days later, after the usual polishings and inspections, the entire camp marched to the School of Instruction to be reviewed by General Maxwell, who presented a number of medals. A week later there was a grand review on the race course by General French, which really was impressive. Our Colonel was in his element.

On St George's Day the battalion enjoyed the Northumberland Fusiliers' traditional honour, which decreed that every member should wear a red and white rose in his hat, and after the Colonel's parade we were all dismissed for sports. There was another occasion when normal routine was suspended because of the arrival of the first batch of 'square heads' (as we sometimes called our German prisoners) to inaugurate the prisoners' camp which had just been completed. One day I was detailed for a twenty-four-hour regimental quarter guard and I knew that I had graduated again. This spell of meticulous smartness and attention to guard duty etiquette was lightened by the prospect of draft leave, a brief respite of six days to say my last farewells.

This short leave, which happened to coincide with the Easter holiday, was marred by the absence of Grace, on a brief visit to Eastbourne. That I did not attempt to follow her to the coast shows how firmly I was gripped by convention. In my old age I have little patience with the youth's lack of initiative. Yet the position could not have been easy, for there was a chronic lack of funds and considerable risk in travelling anywhere in uniform without a pass. We were not permitted to wear civilian clothes and, anyhow, I must have outgrown mine during my spell of army life, nor would I have felt comfortable in company without the military camouflage. I lacked initiative and personality and had not the pen to reach the romantic ideal for which I yearned. Had I been less diffident, I might somehow have redressed the balance at that vital hour.

Yet when bank holiday came — my day to return north — even though I had nothing in particular to do, I rebelled against the unreasonableness of returning when others were enjoying themselves. By extending my furlough by one day I would at least give myself an extra night in bed. Thus it was in the spirit of revolt against the impartial operation of army rules that, for the first and last time during my military service, I, with premeditation, broke the law. In the circumstances to be absent without leave could be a most serious matter; yet not serious enough, I hoped, to justify the absurdity of travelling back on a public holiday. In fact I was, though I did not realise it, revolting against much more than mere bureaucratic thoughtlessness.

On the road from Catterick Station that evening I passed a draft bound for France and waved to a man from my own hut who had gone on leave with me. At that moment it occurred to me that I had perpetrated the greatest villainy. I was placed under open arrest as soon as I arrived. At 7.30 a.m. the following morning I reported to the Orderly Room, cap off and acting the penitent. My punishment — six days C.B. (confined to barracks) and the loss of two days pay under Royal Warrant — was mere routine. If this was the just measure of my particular crime I thought that the protest had been well worth while and rather regretted I had not taken longer, as some others had done. C.B., apart from confinement to the camp, meant attending defaulters each evening and during Saturday afternoon, when we were given extra fatigues, cleaning up, digging, cook-house duties and the like, but in view of the general policy at the camp of making our lives miserable, defaulters in fact added little extra pain to our days.

As it happened there was a longer gap than usual before the next draft left a fortnight later, and another week before my turn came. I received a new pay book, with a will form to be completed; a field dressing with small capsule of iodine to insert in the special lining pocket of my tunic; and a new identification disk, showing my recently allocated number 292669, which was to remain suspended about my neck until the end of the war.

At one of these last preparatory parades a new man, Harold Eldred, was assigned to the draft. He had only just come out of hospital after a serious illness and looked far from fit. But there was a gap to be filled and this was the easiest way out, a repetition of the process that had put me on that last working party before Christmas. I felt indignant at the obvious injustice of this move and my heart went out to the newcomer whom I decided to take under my wing.

Belatedly, on the day before our departure from Catterick, an effort was made to lift the mantle of oppression. In the afternoon a special dinner was laid for the draft with a certain ceremony and semblance of good fellowship. But the gesture came too late and the show fell flat. We knew full well that our home-bound colleagues had done their damndest to prepare us as lambs for the slaughter and there was no love lost on either side. My mind went back inevitably to that other ceremony at Harrogate the previous summer, when sympathy and goodwill had been in the ascendant. Then our hearts had been overflowing: at this second banquet the traditional soldier's farewell was exemplified. We were going on this occasion in duty bound, but with hard hearts and few illusions.

On the following afternoon, at 4.00 p.m. precisely, the Colonel addressed us on parade, saying farewell in words that at least suggested kindliness. We marched to the station at Catterick Bridge to the strains of our regimental band and thence were played away with 'The British Grenadiers'. But there were no friendly faces to bid us farewell and the make-believe, if well-intentioned, left a hollow feeling within us.

A NOTE TO THE READER

If you have enjoyed this book enough to leave a review on **Amazon** and **Goodreads**, then we would be truly grateful.
The Estate of Norman Gladden

Sapere Books is an exciting new publisher of brilliant fiction and popular history.

To find out more about our latest releases and our monthly bargain books visit our website: **saperebooks.com**